GETTING SENT

A Relational Approach to Support Raising

PETE SOMMER

InterVarsity Press
Downers Grove, Illinois

InterVarsity Press
P.O. Box 1400, Downers Grove, IL 60515
World Wide Web: www.ivpress.com
E-mail: mail@ivpress.com

InterVarsity Press®is the book-publishing division of InterVarsity Christian Fellowship/USA®, a student movement active on campus at hundreds of universities, colleges and schools of nursing in the United States of America, and a member movement of the International Fellowship of Evangelical Students. For information about local and regional activities, write Public Relations Dept., InterVarsity Christian Fellowship/USA, 6400 Schroeder Rd., P.O. Box 7895, Madison, WI 53707-7895.

All Scripture quotations, unless otherwise indicated, are taken from the Holy Bible, New International Version® NIV®. Copyright ©1973, 1978, 1984 by International Bible Society. Used by permission of Zondervan Publishing House. All rights reserved.

Cover illustration: Andy Roberts/Tony Stone Images

ISBN 0-8308-2218-6

Printed in the United States of America ♾

Library of Congress Cataloging-in-Publication Data

Sommer, Pete, 1949-
    Getting sent : a relational approach to support raising / Pete Sommer.
        p.   cm.
    ISBN 0-8308-2218-6 (pbk. : alk. paper)
    1. Missions—Finance.   2. Church fund raising.   I Title.
    BV2081.S65 1999   *99 -34679*
    254'.8—dc21   *CIP*

15   14   13   12   11   10   9   8   7   6   5   4   3   2   1

10   09   08   07   06   05   04   03   02   01   00   99

*to Maria
sent with me*

Acknowledgments

While the defects of this book are my sole responsibility, its strengths come from many sources. Above all I must acknowledge Dr. Bill Hautt, founder of Focus Consultants of Alameda, California. Bill took me by the hand in 1982 and said, "Here's how," forever changing my life and ministry.

Barry McLeish, vice president of McConkey-Johnson Consulting, was willing to use his encyclopedic knowledge of fundraising and organizational trends to keep me in touch with reality. Through Barry I discovered that though it's hard to watch your beautiful theories get murdered by ugly facts, the truth does set you free.

Barry Smith, Silicon Valley consultant extraordinaire, labored over difficult sections of the text until even I could understand what I was trying to say.

Noel Becchetti, president of Center for Student Missions, and Andy Hartwell of Bayshore Christian Ministries provided applications of the principles to fundraising for urban causes.

Geneva Vollrath, formerly a Young Life Regional Director, was a constant source of information for the funding of high school ministry in urban and suburban areas. Geneva also gets my thanks in her role today as InterVarsity's vice president for development for generously granting me the time to finish the book.

Time to do the main draft was granted by the first champion of this book, Bob Fryling, then director of InterVarsity's campus ministries. It was the latest iteration in Bob's commitment to integrate training into InterVarsity and make it a learning organization.

Donna Wilson, my colleague in training at InterVarsity, wrote the women's chapter out of her own effective ministry, but she is no mere "niche" consultant. She has helped over the years to refine our total development training program. InterVarsity's Paul Tokunaga guided my attempts to place the book in context for Asian-American readers. His questions were inconvenient, frustrating and very fruitful.

Daryl K. Anderson, associate director for finance and development at Evangelical Free Church Mission, was kind enough to read the entire draft and render it more useful for overseas-bound missionaries.

Reverend Rick Langeloh of Menlo Park Presbyterian Church and Tim Halls of both Latin America Mission and the Walnut Creek Presbyterian Church let me distill some of their insights into the text. They offer experience in sustaining ongoing support of over three hundred ministries and evaluating thousands of financial requests.

Thanks also to the Yuban Coffee Company, whose product maintained me at the keyboard into the late hours.

Three people have shaped the values that I hope guide the book. The first is Larry Langdon, who flunked retirement by completing his job as vice president for corporate tax, licensing and customs at Hewlett-Packard and is now division commissioner for large and midsize business at the Internal Revenue Service. Larry is currently chair of the board of Fuller Theological Seminary and president of the Lowell Berry Foundation. Larry has been my friend and mentor through the years on issues of training, personal and organizational development, finance and ethics. He crystallized my mission: "Your ministry is to give your ministry away." This book is one effort to do that.

Second is my beloved late father, Harry J. Sommer, through whose generosity to missions his four children learned the blessedness of giving. He was an adult convert, and he never got over the offer of God's grace in the gospel of Jesus Christ. He spent his best energy using his gifts to extend that offer to people around the world. Our home was something of a missionary hotel, the site of regular prayer meetings in which my parents would join other friends for times of extended prayer.

Finally, my thanks for inspiration and wisdom to my wife Maria, who found Christ while she was an international student at New Mexico State and served with InterVarsity in Kansas and California. Raised in poverty, she has taught me that giving money can destroy people as well as empower them and that life does not consist in the abundance of our possessions. Above all, she has raised two children who believe that getting sent to proclaim the kingdom of God represents the life worth living.

Introduction

I got off to a rough start in raising support. I was fresh out of college and eager to share Christ on campus. Two hundred of my parents' friends received my request letter. In spite of my fervent prayers, a good letter and a clear request, only three people returned my response card. *They know my need, and they have the money. Maybe they aren't concerned about the campus. Maybe they don't think I'm the person for the job.* I sensed I was breaking some mysterious rules, but what were they? How did you find out? Maybe God was telling me I'd missed his will or had some unconfessed sin in my life. I didn't get it.

Getting Sent aims to demystify support raising. It draws on hundreds of interviews, seminars and sixteen organizations who put missionaries on campuses, in cities and overseas. The people who work in these agencies differ by personality, race and social and educational background. We've observed them to define the what, why, who and how of forming a support team.

Getting Sent is written primarily to men and women in their twenties, college graduates who are new missionaries or mission candidates. It's also useful for the increasing number of midlife believers crossing over into missions from the marketplace, teaching or government. The mission may be to the campus or the city, rural or overseas, through a small or large agency. The book aims at someone who has been a Christian at least five years and is responsible to raise fifteen to eighty thousand dollars annually from his or her own sources.

As missionaries we aren't self-appointed or self-sufficient. Our call to mission work is validated through God's people who give their gifts to send us to our work. Part of that call is asking people for those gifts. *Fundraising* is the common term for that, but a more descriptive word is *development.* Some call it "friendraising," "people raising," "resource de-velopment" or "support team building." All of these terms rightly focus on the person who gives rather than methods for how to "get a gift."

Development is about two people, missionary and donor, each using their gifts to meet the same need. That need may be to lead college students to Christ, to empower disadvantaged city youth, to bring health services to the poor or spiritual healing to the hurt, to introduce Christ to those who have never heard of him or to provide Christian camping opportunities for handicapped kids. Your task is to discover how God is calling your friend and to share how he has called you. Your work and your relationships with these individuals and their resources must evolve together. Simply put, the concept is to

form a group of people who will surround your ministry with prayer and resource it according to their interest and ability.

Getting Sent lays out a procedure for forming such a group. At the start the strategy is time-intensive, then it tapers off to ten percent of your time annually. The goal is to free you for ministry, not to turn you into a development professional.

Getting Sent has four basic parts and eighteen short chapters. In each you'll find theory and practical information. You'll find the stories of real people who have done what you are about to do. Each chapter will show you tools you can incorporate into a system to keep you on track. They've been selected for ease of use to allow you to start applying the theory in a short time. Each chapter ends with a summary of the key concept.

Working through the book in a small group will be more effective than on your own. Use the book as a supplement to whatever face-to-face training your agency offers.

The relational strategy of this book is not necessarily the quickest way to raise money, but it is the most lasting and fulfilling for those who give and receive. When your ministry pushes you to your limits, you'll find strength in the Lord and the knowledge that he's raised up a special group of people who pray and care for you. You're not out there on your own. By the Lord of the universe and through his people, you've been sent.

Part One
Building the Foundation

Answers to the following questions form
the foundation for building a support team.

What does God think?
What do we think?
What do donors think?

1

God's Word Is Final

Spiritual people don't ask for money. They pray and God moves people to give."

"Christians should give only to a local church."

"Paul worked at a job so he wouldn't have to raise support. You should too."

"Your organization should raise funds for you."

"Personal support is not biblical. We should give to the cause only."

"Raise support? You have to be a great salesman to succeed."

When you raise support, you'll hear these comments. Where would you go in the Bible to back up what you do? Christians claim biblical support for each of the following support raising patterns:

☐ Simply pray about your needs.

☐ Pray about your needs and report on your ministry.

☐ Pray, report on your ministry and answer questions about finances when people ask.

☐ Pray and report on both the ministry and its finances.

☐ Pray, report on the work and its needs and ask people to join the work as givers of both money and other resources.

But saying there is biblical support for all of these approaches doesn't mean any or all of them are right for you or your particular kind of mission. What approach does God want you to take? Resourcing your ministry will mean struggle, whichever you choose. No option guarantees a smooth ride. The way to the promised land is through the wilderness. Struggle is one way God tests our call, to see what is in our hearts.

Remember the long way that the LORD your God has led you these forty years in the wilderness, in order to humble you, testing you to know what was in your heart, whether or not you would keep his commandments. (Deut 8:2 NRSV)

When we struggle it's not enough to think back to our "appointment letter" or say, "That's just the way my organization does it." We need conviction from Scripture. Preparing to debate is not the point. When someone wants to argue theology, they are probably not going to be our donor. When Paul describes the Scriptures as "God-breathed" (2 Tim 3:16), his Greek word for *breathed* echoes the Hebrew in Genesis 2 where the Lord breathes life into Adam (Gen 2:7). God breathes life into us through his Word and makes us equal to the struggle.

Scripture has dos, don'ts and norms. There is neither command nor prohibition in the Bible for missionaries to form personal support teams. The norm in Scripture for ministry is that both God and our donor are best served when we pray, report and ask him or her directly to give the needed resources. That's how we get sent. We'll lay out the foundation for this conviction in Bible studies between chapters.

STUDY ONE: GOD THE PROVIDER—ISRAEL'S BEGINNING

Deuteronomy 8: Moses' Explanation of the Wilderness Journey
☐ *What are the Lord's main commands in the chapter?*
☐ *What did he want Israel to learn by wandering in the desert (vv. 2-6)?*
☐ *What does he now promise (vv. 7-10)?*

☐ *What are his warnings (vv. 11-20)?*
☐ *How are you in a similar position to the Israelites?*

1 Kings 17:1-16: The Lord's Provision During Depression

☐ *What would your reaction be if you were Elijah when the brook went dry?*
☐ *What happened as a result of his direct requests for help?*
☐ *What does this story reveal about the Lord's care and power over "the economy"?*
☐ *When were you sure of something God called you to do, but it looked impossible? What did you do? What happened?*
☐ *When it happens again (a certainty), what should you do?*

> *I realized that I had this fear that my donors controlled what was going to happen with my support more than God. The principle that God is the provider has carried over into my attitude about who is actually in control. It's been a key in the whole support-raising process: an attitude of thankfulness for another opportunity to trust God.*
>
> *After several requests and nos I actually felt a peace. It was almost exciting because now in my mind there was nobody, I'd exhausted my resources. It was as if the Lord was saying to me, "Let me show you what I'm going to do."* (Donna, campus worker in Arizona, now raises a budget of more than $45,000.)

2

The Fear
Factor

I t was my second year in campus ministry. I went downtown to meet
an influential Christian businessman. I parked my car. I got out
and looked up at a gleaming office tower. As I waited at the curb
for the light to change, my palms got wet and my mouth got dry, and
I thought, this would be an excellent time to get hit by a truck.

Rich, a gifted young pastor, interviewed with a mission in inner-city
Chicago. Rich and the mission's director found great rapport and
agreement on their philosophy of ministry and the job. Then the
director explained, "You'll be required to raise fifty percent of your
funding." Rich turned white. "You would have thought we'd invited him
to the guillotine."

Anne was in a training seminar in Dallas. When it came time to
telephone, she picked up the handset, dialed a number and burst into
tears.

Ninety-two percent of all Christian workers experience fear of asking
for money, and the other eight percent are liars. Most of us would rather
have a root canal. This chapter won't serve professional fundraisers who

already live to sell. I learn all I can from such people, but I could no more be one of them than golf like Tiger Woods. I am a missionary with no business background who deals with this issue only because there's no way around it. Missionaries would rather shop at thrift stores and eat peanut butter for dinner than ask for money.

How does fear stop us and what can we do about it?

FEAR'S FORMS

Hearing a No
☐ There are only a few people I can ask. They make or break my joining the mission. If they don't say yes I'll never make it.

☐ People don't want to be approached. When I call for an appointment I'm imposing on them.

☐ I risk the friendship when I bring up the subject of support.

Hearing a Yes
☐ I feel undeserving and guilty for taking someone's money to do something I enjoy.

☐ It's unfair for me to take without giving them something in return: I win; they lose. Being unfair makes me feel lousy about myself.

☐ This is not a *real* job. I'm not really contributing to society.

Shame
☐ I'm begging. Asking for money goes against everything I've been taught.

☐ I will look foolish to my church community and friends.

☐ My parents will be humiliated if I ask for money.

Culture affects the way we express shame. Blue collar people feel offense to their pride at "not pulling their own weight." Young professionals hear that they are throwing away their privileges. Black missionaries sometimes think they will be seen as welfare cases when approaching white donors. Asian-Americans get the message that they are shaming the family by asking for what a good family should provide.

People of every color and class are unhappy about the whole thing.

Different versions of the shame message include men should become pastors or businessmen not parachurch workers, women should not be in full-time ministry at all, who cares about college students anyway, why waste your time on those hopeless kids, you should do something your parents can be proud of, why are you joining a white church and leaving our community, and don't you *dare* ask any of the relatives.

We'll deal in turn with the fear of the no, the fear of the yes and the issue of shame.

WHAT DOESN'T WORK

Feel behind in your paperwork? Schedule a day for support raising. Amazing how we have to file those reports, drink another cup of coffee and dust the ficus before we can pick up that telephone.

> *I blocked out time to make phone calls. I made lists of people to ask. I analyzed contributions with a spreadsheet program. I reviewed my training manual. I sent out letters telling people I would phone them about the cause. I looked at the phone, and I just couldn't pick up the receiver. I guess you can't organize your way out of fear.*

If just knowing the biblical basis would do it, our best Bible scholars would be our greatest fundraisers. Alas, not so. A powerful time of prayer can carry us for a season, but we often wind up in the same rut. Doing phone calls as a group effort is great, but most of the time we're going to be on our own.

PESSIMISTS AND OPTIMISTS

So where *do* we go with our fears? We can't just wish them away, and yes, God *can* heal us. Barry McLeish states it clearly: *The solution to fear is conviction about the cause.* When we have that, we fight our fears. They don't disappear, but they lose a lot of their power.

Conviction about our call and cause will move us to find weapons for that fight. One weapon is the thesis of Martin Seligman's *Learned Optimism*.[1] Seligman observes that some people are more fearful than others. They think that bad events, such as refusals of their requests, are personal, pervasive (or universal) and permanent. Major consequences follow. We've adapted one of Seligman's illustrations to show how this might look in a nonprofit but secular setting.

Picture Alan and Sarah, fundraisers for two environmental organizations. One of their duties is to call people on the agency mailing lists and ask them for contributions.

Alan calls a name. After fifteen seconds the person hangs up. A second call comes to a polite no. A third call results in a thirty-minute conversation, then Alan discovers the person he is talking to is unemployed, lonely and just wants to talk. A fourth call: "Stop it, you creep." Click. Alan is completely frustrated by this adversity. He gives up, gets a beer and sits down to watch TV. He sends himself three basic messages: *I'm no good at this, I'm a failure,* and *I can't stand the thought of this day after day; it will never improve.* He sees the situation as

personal
pervasive
permanent

Sarah has the same experience with her first four calls. But she keeps going. Nothing changes through call eleven, but on the twelfth call she gets a yes. When Sarah finishes, she thinks, *It's too bad some people won't look at what we're accomplishing, it was not the best day to call,* and *in the future I'll be sure to mention that I'm a young mom, and I understand how people on tight budgets struggle to give to causes they believe in.*

Whereas Alan sees his situation as *personal, pervasive and permanent,* Sarah sees hers as

nonpersonal
specific
temporary

Alan is a classic pessimist; Sarah is a classic optimist. Up through call number four, they have the same experiences, but their *interpretations differ radically.* At the root of Alan's pessimism is a belief—not a fact. He believes he is *helpless.* Sarah sees things that are beyond her control, but she also sees *steps she can take to reduce the chance of more bad sessions.*

Such three-dimensional pessimism and optimism Seligman calls our *explanatory style*—how we talk to ourselves about our success or failure. He confesses there are born optimists such as Sarah; then there are the rest of us. The Sarahs of this world become successful because their explanatory style leads them to persevere. Alan wrongly thinks that Sarah is optimistic because she's successful at fundraising. In fact, Sarah is successful *because she is optimistic enough to make twenty calls, five times more than Alan.* Since most of us are more like Alan, Seligman says it is necessary to consciously dispute our pessimism with facts.

At this point, Seligman's insight converges with Scriptural truth. God calls us to *remember, consider, think upon, and reckon* the great facts of God's character revealed in his story and then to examine our own story in the light of his. Let's proceed with the dispute.

Disputing Pessimism with the Facts

The fact is, God is your provider, not the donor. If the God who loves us wants our work funded, he'll provide through people we know or others we won't meet until he decides it's time. Most people haven't rejected our appeal; they haven't even heard about our ministry.

Because the Holy Spirit has already prepared certain people to respond, our job is *not to persuade people but to discover them.*

As we come to believe that God is our true provider, we gain more freedom to risk our relationships. Asking risks the relationship but can also deepen it. Consider the fact that you won't even be in touch with your pal in a few years if he doesn't give to your work. You'll move, he'll move, and you will grow apart. But if he commits to help your cause, you'll stay in touch. Asking and risking will often help you *keep* a relationship.

The fact is, if you enjoy your work, you are more, not less, deserving of support. You are hardworking, employable and worthy of a living wage. We are called to suffer at times, but not incessantly. The weakness of our old logic becomes clear when we ask, Is the world a better place if I do something I *don't* enjoy?

The fact is, you are not a problem—you're a solution. Consider the donor's perspective: they have causes but lack the time, gifts, temperament or call to do it themselves. By funding your work they become coworkers in the inner city, on campus or in the country where you go.

It's a matter of each part of the body doing what it was designed to do to bring about the progress of God's kingdom.

Because their work is needed, the number of nonprofit organizations in the United States has tripled in twenty years to almost 700,000. Thousands of scientists, artists, dancers, teachers, musicians, disaster relief workers, medical doctors, contractors, psychologists and businesspersons are learning how to find patrons and raise funds on top of their other duties. Many thousands more want to do something about the problems they see every day but can't address. Your ministry comes to them as a solution.

The fact is, mission work is no basis for shame, and we can win over at least some of the skeptics. Let's consider "begging," parents, race and class. First, understand in the words of the hymn, "this world is not a friend of grace." From an eternal perspective, your opposition is not about being black, white, Asian, rich, poor, male or female. It's triggered by your commitment to Jesus Christ. If respectability is your goal, don't be a missionary. Are you ashamed of building a support team, or are you ashamed of him and the gospel (Rom 1:16)?

Does Asking Equal Begging?
From the Epistles we can see that Paul didn't think so. Some missionaries see their work as begging because *they think funds only go to them instead of through them.* Now hear this: It's not about you. You are *not* the primary beneficiary of your donor's gift. If you just need money, quit your ministry now and get a new job, because you have the talent to pull down a higher paycheck. We ask for resources of all kinds so we can be free to do something urgently needed for children or students or people in trouble. An urban missionary says that when he has these negative feelings, "I view the problem as being me, and I've lost track of the big

picture—my feelings of personal comfort outweigh the needs of the organization and its people, in which I genuinely believe." Confidence is not a word that springs to mind when I think of this young leader, but conviction is. His conviction has freed him to deal with his fears.

When you have conviction, you do *not* say, "Please give to my support." You ask, "Would you join a team of people who will surround this ministry with prayer and help to fund it?" The money (and time, expertise and other gifts) will go *through* you *to* others. You ask for them because they can't, and you are convinced that the love of Jesus Christ, in whatever form you deliver it, is what they need.

Parents. Try marketing before martyrdom. Can you arrange for your parents to come down and see where you will work, meet the boss and see that these people are kind of normal? Is there someone who supports your mission that they respect? Can your supervisor visit them to answer questions? What do they really know about your agency? Ask your agency to host a reception for parents of their younger staff. This can reassure everyone involved and be fun. Walk in the light with them (1 Jn 1:7).

Consider also that your folks know you better than you do. So even if you can't reconcile their wishes with your intent to work for a Christian organization, look for the truth in their criticism, and do what you can to keep communication open. "Listen, my son, to your father's instruction and do not forsake your mother's teaching" (Prov 1:8). Celebrate what you do have in common. If communication on your career choice has broken down, find an issue that's less tense (two on a scale of ten), and see if you can work through that disagreement. Build up a history of disagreeing, listening and loving. Once parents see how God is working in your life, they can change.

"Your father will not be giving to your financial support," said my mother. My dad was so opposed to the idea of asking for money at our Chinese church that he wouldn't talk to me. When asked by his friends what I would be doing, he was ashamed to acknowledge it. If there were a time in my life when I felt rejected by my dad, that would be it. However, what I thought was a fundraising death sentence was the start of God's provision. For the first few weeks, we didn't talk; for the next few, we

argued. He consented to my decision by the third month but would still not support my work.

Meanwhile, my mom became my biggest fundraiser at church. She arranged for me to meet with people, and I shared about God's work on campus. After a slow start, I was at forty percent of budget. Dad was watching and seeing how God moved people to give. During month six, one of his closest friends committed to give fifteen percent of my whole budget. Wow! God seemed to change my dad's mind. Perhaps it was his friend's generosity. Perhaps he didn't want to be outdone by someone else. Whatever it was, he sent a check and his blessing for over twenty percent of my need. Over the next three years, his support increased while I served in that ministry.

Not all stories end so happily, but remember, your parents care more about you than your organization does. Not more than *God* does but more than your *agency* does, because organizations—by definition—don't "care." They are vehicles to live out your call. They may even be communities, but they are temporary. So obey the Lord but honor your parents within that defining commitment. If this is your issue, take advantage of the book *Following Jesus Without Dishonoring Your Parents* (InterVarsity Press, 1998).

Race. "Why did you join that white church?" It may not be said out loud, but you get the idea. The African-American community has reason to ask the question because it is used to seeing its upwardly mobile people depart. When the question comes up, you want the leadership of your church to speak up for you. Your church may think of mission strictly within their own communities. If so, you can demonstrate how your work is part of the solution to problems they experience, first with your pastor or other leaders.

How do you explain what you do? If you're going to do university ministry, the words "staff" or "campus minister" may mean nothing, so refer to yourself as the "program director" or "assistant program director" and to your core group as "volunteers." Talk about how the program addresses needs: keeping our young people in the church, helping them academically, imparting witnessing and leadership skills, and volunteering in the community. With your organization's help, harmonize your vocabulary with that of your audience. "I found that telling people about how God is changing and saving lives on campus is like what Paul used in his defense in 2 Corinthians 3:2-3," says an African-American staff worker.

Show support for the leaders of your local church. When you first start to think about joining a mission agency, invite their counsel. Get the most senior representative of your mission that you can to meet with them. Seek the blessing of (1) a leader in your church, (2) an advocate within the congregation, and (3) a successful model—for instance, another missionary from your church. Aim for the goal that your leaders would recommend you to the congregation for support.

If you're a nonwhite worker or missionary, you may feel awkward about soliciting support from interested white men, women, churches and foundations. Realize that while you may see asking as a problem, many in the white community see your actions as a solution. White donors get approached for funds without ceasing, so it's no big deal when you share with them about your cause. From their viewpoint you're doing nothing unusual, and you have more credibility than many.

Class. Does the lifestyle of wealthy Christians create a barrier for you? For many missionaries the country club and the executive office are Jesus-free zones. But consider the words of this Brazilian-born urban missionary.

> *For years I shunned the company of financially successful people and felt real righteous about it. For sure, they were compromising their faith by going to the marketplace, while I truly understood the gospel and led a simpler life. I see now that I had the problem. I lacked the inner spiritual strength to hang with people different from me. My lack of personal strength meant I could only socialize with people who shared my views. Now I understand that each person stands before the Lord, not me. They have made different choices than me, but now I'm free to be a bridge between their community and mine.*

If you come from privilege, you'll see your friends quickly climb the corporate ladder while you struggle. Parents may feel awkward telling their friends at the country club what you do, but it's not hopeless. A young lady from Stanford "threw away" her expensive education to do youth work. As she sat in the study of a lovely home, calling people for support appointments, her mother finally took notice. She observed that her daughter was doing a solid professional job, and she remarked, "Maybe this makes sense after all." That was less than a Christian blessing, but it was respect for quality work, and she became less skeptical.

Faith Exercises

Here are the four practices which will help you receive God's gifts for overcoming fear.

1. Bible meditation. Read slowly and reflect on one or more of the following texts. You may find it helpful to sit with a friend or small group and read a text aloud three times, letting truth echo in the soul. After hearing a passage, allow a period of silence to think over what God has said.

Texts for Meditation

God's promises to provide for those he calls

Genesis 12:1-9	Isaiah 41:8-10
Exodus 3—4	Mark 1:16-20; 3:13-19
Deuteronomy 8	John 15:12-17
Joshua 1:1-9	Acts 1:8; 13:44-47; 26:12-23
1 Kings 17:8-16	

Handling anxiety in fundraising

Exodus 20:2-4	Matthew 28
Psalm 55:22	Luke 18:1-8
Isaiah 55:10-11	2 Corinthians 4:1-15
Jeremiah 1	1 Timothy 4:14

The validity of support for ministry

Numbers 18:21-24	2 Timothy 1:3-7
Luke 8:3; 10:7	1 Peter 4:7-11
1 Corinthians 16:5-6	

He who did not spare his own Son but gave him up for us all, will he not also give us all things with him? (Rom 8:32 RSV)

Question 1: *What is your only comfort in life and in death?*

Answer: *That I with body and soul, both in life and in death, am not my own, but belong unto my faithful Savior Jesus Christ, who, with his precious blood, has fully satisfied for all my sins, and delivered me from all the power of the devil; and so preserves me that without the will of my heavenly Father, not a hair can fall from my head; yes, that all things must be subservient to my salvation, and therefore, by his Holy Spirit he also assures me of eternal life, and makes me sincerely willing and ready, henceforth, to live unto Him.* (The Heidelberg Catechism, 1563)

2. Group prayer. "If two of you on earth agree about anything you ask for, it will be done for you by my Father.... For where two or three come together in my name, there am I with them" (Mt 18:19).

Jesus tells us that he will do something when we pray together that he will not do when we pray alone. Find two or three people outside your agency who will pray with you for your financial need. For six months gather once a month or more if possible. Ask one of them to keep a record of what God does.

Read two or three prayer letters or ministry reports with stories about changed lives. Thank God for each of the people who have joined your support team. Look at your own prayer list of people touched by your ministry.

I had to get so in debt that I was in a desperate situation. Most people don't need to do that! I sent a clear letter, with personal remarks on each. I did the basics—phoning, thank-you notes and follow up. But I also sought prayer. I prayed through my letter list, and I gathered people to pray for me. I confronted my own use of inappropriate coping. This is part of my spiritual development. (a missionary to nursing students in Ohio)

I went through a year of hard personal circumstances that left me with little emotional drive to do fundraising. My efforts were marginal, and the situation became intolerable. I began to ask people to pray for my situation, which I had been reluctant to do before. It was prayer, a training seminar and being willing to speak up that made the difference. Though we have to learn the mechanics, building a support team is mostly prayer, not technique. (campus staff worker from Wisconsin)

3. Meetings without money. How can you learn to meet the financial leaders who will help you in bigger ways? Gear up by first learning to get appointments where money is not on the line. Seek meetings with leaders in your community just to get acquainted. If you're a campus worker, go for a short appointment with the president or the dean, or as high up as you can reach. Request fifteen minutes to ask a few questions.

☐ What are your concerns or priorities as (title) on this campus?
☐ What's your perspective on the religious groups on this campus?
☐ What contribution do you feel they could make?
☐ Would you ever be available to speak to our chapter or have a meeting with our student leaders?
☐ Were you ever personally active in a campus religious group?
☐ What are your concerns about race relations on this campus?

Cathy, an InterVarsity staffworker in the Plains states, sensed an impression from the Lord during a quiet time one morning. He seemed to say, "I want you to meet with the president of the university." Her first response was to resist. *Who am I to call up and ask for a meeting with the president? It's probably just my own ego.* But the thought returned. *What shall I say?* Realizing that this might be the Lord speaking, she changed her prayer, asking for discernment, wisdom and boldness. She made the phone call that day and was given a time to meet.

After introductions and small talk Cathy asked the president, "What's your greatest concern about this campus?" He answered immediately, "Racial tension. We have a serious problem, and we need to do something before it gets out of control." Cathy hid her amazement. "That's our priority this year in InterVarsity," she explained and described steps the chapter was taking to build bridges of racial reconciliation. She invited him to speak to the group, and he gladly accepted. At the close of the meeting, Cathy offered to pray for him and the campus.

Cathy sang with the African-American Gospel Choir on campus. The president and his wife attended their concert soon after the meeting with Cathy. Afterward the president's wife came up to Cathy and asked, "Are you the one who offered to pray for my husband? No one has ever done that before. Thank you!" Cathy's responsiveness to God's voice gave the campus ministry favor in the eyes of the administration. It was not calculated. There was no fundraising agenda. It was done in obedience and blessed by God. But it empowered her for her other tasks.

If you're working in a city, unlike the campus, you will probably not be the point person for the ministry. You have an advantage over your campus counterpart in that you likely have supervision of one kind or another in the same city. Ask your mission if you can accompany a board member or a leader who is paying a visit to someone who leads the political structures, school district or some other service agency in the community. You will benefit in information, practice of key skills and acculturation to the leadership in your community.

God's Word makes it plain that we are to both reach down to the needy and up to the powerful. Leaders should know that Christians are active in their communities (Is 60:3; Acts 9:15; 26:26).

4. Walk with the wise. "He who walks with the wise grows wise" (Prov 13:20). A relational strategy is more caught than taught. Follow your own mission's development representatives on a few days of their own work. Or get outside your mission and spend a couple of days with another missionary. See what she does, follow her on appointments if she'll let you, meet a few of her friends and ask her advice. List the questions she asks people and the questions that are asked of her. You'll learn from her success, mistakes and faith. You'll learn more about who gives, and why, in your own community. Go on appointments with a more experienced person several times during the first few months of your service and a minimum of once a year thereafter.

Just as we catch new abilities from keeping the right company, we also get unhelpful traits from running with negative people. When the pessimists in your organization gather around the coffee station for their usual un-happy hour, skip the meeting.

WRAP

Dispute your fears with the facts. The basic fact of life is the authority of Jesus Christ as Lord. Our adversity is not personal, pervasive or permanent; in fact, it's part of his plan. God knew what he was doing when he created you and called you to ministry. Each unique trait of personality, family, class, gender and ethnicity is useful and valuable to his kingdom. Train yourself in godliness with the help of the exercises (1 Tim 4:7).

When I phone to ask for money, my heart still beats a little faster. Sometimes I still get tongue-tied. But my conviction about my call is stronger and frees me to risk what is temporary for what has eternal value.

Building a support team is not risk-free, but you'll grow like crazy trying. Our Lord just says, "Follow me." Alan or Sarah may serve a good cause, but you are engaged in the ultimate cause and one that gives a base from which all the other good causes develop. You serve the King. When this fact grips you, you may have fears, but you won't let them rob you of life.

STUDY TWO: GOD THE PROVIDER—THE EXILE

Isaiah 41:8-20: God's Glory and Our Welfare
The Jews were in exile in Babylon, and many had lost hope for return. Those who were free to return feared a loss of economic security in Babylon.
☐ *Why does God want to provide for his servants (v. 20, compare 40:5; 43:7)?*
☐ *God's deepest motive is to glorify himself as mighty and merciful. A word study of "glory" reveals its frequent tie to mercy (Ex 33:18—34:7; Ps 50:15; Jn 17). How does it affect you to know that he ties your welfare to his glory?*
☐ *Put your name in every reference to Jacob or Israel and receive this as God's word to you today through Jesus Christ.*

3

Why
People Give

Our ministry changed her life. She is financially successful. She
has friends on our staff who call and visit. She never gives to
our work. I don't get it.

*He owns the Toyota dealership, two huge homes and three luxury
cars, and he skis in Europe. He's an elder in church. When we finally
got in to see him and asked for his help, he gave us $100. I don't get it.*

*I met this man at a church potluck. He seemed interested in what I
did, so I asked for a time to meet. He'd never heard of our ministry. We
spent an hour over breakfast, and he gave me a check for $1,000. I still
don't get it!*

Why do people give? In the next few pages we will try to dispel some
myths and establish a few principles about what motivates men and
women to partner with causes.

NINE MYTHS AND SEVEN TRUTHS

Myth One: People Give Because They Can Afford It

"Mr. Robbins owns the Lexus dealership. If we can tell him our story, he will give a large gift." We make the mistake of thinking that wealth and concern go hand in hand. Research shows that eight of ten who make at least one million dollars annually leave no money to causes in their wills.[1] A Gallup survey said the weakest segment of donors in the United States were those with incomes of $40,000 to $100,000 a year.[2] People don't give because they "have the money."

Myth Two: A Big Bash Means Cash

Three hundred fifty people crammed the banquet hall to hear a famous Christian politician speak on behalf of a mission to high-school students. "We had the biggest crowd; we got the fewest dollars of any dinner. People came for the speaker, not our cause," rued the director.

New missionaries wish that banquets, golf tournaments, silent auctions or alumni parties would raise big dollars for them. In fact, many big productions fail to cover their own cost. Banquets are labor intensive, can pull you off critical tasks and can leave you and your volunteers exhausted with little to show for it. The right events can work well, but twenty, one-hour conversations are more powerful than twenty hours spent on a big bash. The question is, what kind of event best serves your donor and your mission?

Myth Three: State-of-the-Art Graphics Turn People into Donors

Of course you need good print communication. Just remember that many of the people you approach have seen it all, so unless you're Steven Spielberg you won't surprise them with creativity. Strive for clarity, a few good photos and an uncluttered format.

Myth Four: Since Giving Is Painful, Make It Up to People

Once in a while, sending along a book, article or photo with a personal note is a nice touch. Stuffing boxes to send everyone on your list a mug or T-shirt may make you feel like you are doing something for the donor. In fact, you'll probably look wasteful.

People feel blessed by giving, or they don't give in the first place. The thrill for donors is in seeing your ministry make progress.

Keeping them informed about that is most of the recognition or return they desire.

Myth Five: People Give Because You're in Crisis

"I need $12,000 by December, or I will have to leave my ministry." You can use an appeal like this once in awhile, provided it's true. If used more frequently than that you will get money only from your mom. To everyone else, this kind of letter says that you're a poor manager or that God is out of money (again). Unfortunately, it's standard practice among missionaries to conclude a letter with a paragraph about how far behind budget they are. Reporting on your support progress is fine for your first year, but thereafter you should not talk finances more than twice a year.

Myth Six: You Have to Collect the Gift on the Spot

A high pressure "closer" tries to get a donor to give a specific amount in a face-to-face meeting. He is willing to make him feel disobedient to God if he doesn't give enough and won't take no for an answer. You *can* extract money from people this way, with keen skills and a dull conscience, but you can't get a partnership.

Not once in twenty-six years of support raising have I found it necessary to conclude a meeting with the question, "Is there anything to stop you from writing a check right now?" The need for an immediate yes or no is usually the result of pressure we feel and our own poor planning. You'll be free to trust the people God calls to your team.

Myth Seven: People Give Because of Great Statistics

Our student ministry was bigger than the other campus ministries combined, but we raised the least amount of money. Staff from the other ministries talked about changed *individual* lives, while we recited our activities and the numbers of students who came out to meetings. People care about impact, but impact is best conveyed through a picture, not a number. The good news is that you don't need "bigness," especially at the outset of a ministry, to succeed.

We support your work because we have a personal connection and confidence in you. Most important, we want to make a difference with our giving, so we looked for something small. (an out-of-state donor to a small urban ministry)

Myth Eight: Letters That Ask for Different Amounts Give Donors a Choice

Wouldn't it be cool if everyone would just do their little bit over and over? Then we could move on to the more exciting parts of ministry. Alas, our donors insist on acting as individuals, ignoring our need for efficiency. A small number respond; a smaller number do what we ask; but most just go on their way in silence like the 203 folks who got my first letter.

Myth Nine: Copy Successful Ministries

It's easy to be dazzled by large, well-known agencies. If you want to copy them, however, you should ask yourself why you don't join them. If you're in a small agency in a field with some dominating players—forgive the suggestion that there is competition for donors—you need to have a niche strategy. You can't work another group's strategy better than they do, and it's not your call to try. The Lord doesn't want us to "ape" anyone else or exalt our cause by putting down someone else's.

"What makes your work different than ministry 'X'?" asked the pastor to Robin, a new campus worker in a college town. "I can answer that best," answered Robin, "by sharing about the kind of students God is using our work to reach." In a few brief minutes she described how two students came to commitment to Christ. Her answer conveyed her ministry's distinctives without critiquing other agencies or people.

The question *you* need to answer is, what is *your* focus? Tell people what *your* mission is and who is being changed through it. When you're asked about another ministry, say something positive and add, "I'm really not an expert in what they're doing." You're in good shape if you can also say, "Our leaders meet to share and pray."

Since your ministry is special, your donors will be too. If you speak and act like all the other groups, you won't find your own constituency. It's even liberating when, after a tense relationship with a donor, you can say, "John, it appears that we just aren't your ministry." So be yourself. All gifts come with strings attached; what matters is that those strings are values that you hold in common with your donor. How does that happen?

Why People Give

1. God moves people. Some "sure" people will fail to support you while others you least expect will join your support team. Mystery hovers over the process.

> *Hannah's account was in the red. Her supervisor told her she had to leave her campus ministry for four weeks. She wept. On her way to the meeting, with one final talk to give to her campus group, she strongly sensed the Lord's presence. At the meeting she explained why she needed to be off for a month; then she gave her talk. Afterward a grad student who was not a particular fan of hers offered her a check for $2,000. "God wants me to give you this."*

> *Marlene's ministry in New York City was struggling financially. After months of seeking God, she got two surprises. A music student in her ministry was hired by a major symphony orchestra and pledged $5,000. Her roommate's mother inherited money and wanted to tithe it—another $15,000.*

See the cause and effect? I don't. Why do we often go through lots of work for little gain and then suddenly have abundance fall in our path? Deuteronomy 8 says that we go through deserts to reveal what's in us and to cast us on to the character of the living God. Then we discover, in ways we cannot program, that God is good and knows our need.

2. Your ministry stands for a value personally important to your donor. How do your potential donors see the world? How did they become believers—if they are believers? What is their educational experience? What are their vocations? Do they volunteer anywhere? Do they have children? Where do they spend money, time and talent? What joys and tragedies have they known? People respond to life and make choices based on their values. This applies to their giving as well.

Bill began his presentation with the line, "Before I describe what we do on campus, let me share the values that guide us . . ." He said a few key words about Scripture, prayer, evangelism and developing people. He told two stories of changed lives to illustrate. The Christian executives listening did the rest with their questions. Their passion was for developing leadership in their people too. Bill wanted to share about other programs, but the donors connected with him on his point of developing leaders and kept him there.

If a loved one has had cancer, we give to the Cancer Society. If we've formed a friendship with a Muslim, we care about Muslim missions. If Youth for Christ made an impact at our high school, we'll consider a gift if the local leader asks for help.

Begin with what you know about the person. Family, career, spiritual journey, health and other life experiences, and involvement with other causes all matter. Take Rick and Susan Donor. They get eight to fifteen requests a week by mail and phone. Who gets their gifts and why? First, they are long-term active Christians. Susan leads a Bible study. They tithe out of an income in the low $90,000s. They are in their early forties, each with a master's degree. They give $2,000 to their local church, which they chose in large part because their children like it. Susan came to Christ through Young Life, and they attend the annual Young Life dinner.

Rick and Susan live in a changing suburban neighborhood and care about race relations. So they volunteer with a youth agency several hours a month and give it $1,000 a year. They send $300 to an interracial church they don't attend. Rick's mother was a victim of arthritis, so they write a check once a year to the Arthritis Foundation and send giving envelopes to their neighbors asking the same. They give about $500 a year to various school benefits for their own and neighbors' children and to their nephew who lives two hundred miles away. They both did summer missions back in their college days. They know several missionaries personally and give modestly to them. They make an occasional gift to causes that promote family values and to special needs, such as camp scholarships, that pop up with the ministries they support already.

In a word, their giving flows from their life choices.

3. Your work makes a difference in the lives of people. Rick and Susan care about their world, but with limits on their time, skills and funds, how much can they do about it? How does their gift help advance the values they hold? Sometimes they feel like their friend, Max, an executive of a midsize tech firm:

> *I guess my friend in Honduras is doing good things. We've supported him for years. I just don't know what difference it makes that I write the checks. I feel like I'm giving into the ether.*

Max supports this ministry out of friendship, and he values the rural evangelism his friend does. Max grew up overseas; his father was an executive for a transnational oil corporation. He met Jesus in college. If Max's friend could show him how his giving makes an impact beyond *maintaining,* he might increase his gift. Even the panhandler knows the principle. That's why he asks you for $2.25; so he can get enough for that bus ticket to Bug Tussle, Oklahoma.

Max is much more excited about the urban ministry he gives to, which sends him a request to help send a kid to camp or acquire a computer and then a follow-up reporting on the difference it's made. He knows that he has done something to make things better. This agency has helped him to feel that his gift has made the world a slightly better place. Max needs his missionary friend to complete the statement, *"If my ministry were fully funded, I would be able to . . ."*

In the African-American context there is an even greater desire to know that gifts are making a difference. Calvin O. Pressley lists eight motivations for black Christian giving.[3]

> The giver shares the vision and accepts the values of the church (ministry).
> There is a genuine belief that their lives have been changed or will be changed because of their religious conviction.
> The need for their financial support is obvious or will make a substantial difference.

Their ability to give is properly assessed.

They are confident that their contributions will be managed well.

They are challenged to give sacrificially.

There is recognition of their support with public acknowledgment.

There are concrete results that are visible or demonstrated because of their giving.[4]

What is striking here is that while "values" still leads the list, three of the motives concern making a difference. African-American donors certainly will not long "give into the ether."

Max will give even though his friend doesn't complete the statement. But he would give more if his friend invited him to visit Honduras and showed him what difference a larger gift could make.

4. Your donor knows you or the person asking him. People give to people. James was called to ministry in Russia but came from a church of two hundred with little interest in missions. He moved to Portland and joined a large, missions-minded church. He met with the missions pastor and told him plainly that he needed to build a donor team. The pastor put him in two volunteer roles. He lived simply on a part-time job and delayed going to Russia for a year. Twelve months later the church completed what he lacked in support, and he went to Moscow.

No shortcut exists for building a network where you are known. Finding a church where you can share your vision, meet people and use your gifts is essential. People don't give on our schedule. Trust must first be built. It took James a year, but now he has a support team that will stay with him for a career in missions.

Some people care about your cause but are confused by the number of agencies dealing with your arena of service. "Why don't all the groups working in Watts just get together?" or "There seem to be a lot of campus ministries out there, but you are the person I know" are comments we often hear from busy people. They don't have the time to compare organizations, but they may meet with you. When they've gained confidence in you and your organization, they will help.

The appointment was set up via phone by a friend. The prospect didn't know me. He was excited about our work, and I asked him to join our support team. He said, No, but told me to keep in touch. That hurt, but I did it. I visited twice a year for two years and then asked again. He wrote a check for $1,200 and said he was sold on the vision and sold on me. (African-American campus minister)

5. They are included and have a sense of ownership. Each donor will define ownership differently. What kind of relationship do they want with the causes they support? Do they volunteer? Do they expect to meet with leaders once in awhile, hear from people affected by the organization or get regular newsletters? Donors view themselves as giving you more than money. While some will leave it there, others will offer wisdom, perspective, skill, experience, time and ideas that can be very helpful.

We chose your ministry because it gives us the chance to meet the people engaged in it. We expect to get that opportunity once in awhile. (retired business couple near a university)

This retired couple is a fount of wisdom for the campus missionaries they support. He was an executive in a major accounting firm and served as treasurer for his large church. They handled difficult people, put three children through college and were lifelong volunteers in their communities. They know scores of missionaries, and they have far more to give than dollars.

Each donor has her own definition of ownership. Don't be afraid to suggest what you seek in the relationship, but be sure you're listening for what is meaningful to her.[5] For that reason, we don't like the popular term *friendraising*. It excludes those who, like the busy individual above, already have a full social life but seek reliable people to whom they can direct their giving. Friendraising can also put our personality, rather than the mission, in first place. "The danger," writes Daryl Anderson of Evangelical Free Church Missions, "is to think every donor is a friend or every friend should be a donor."

Many donors already are your friends, and many more will become friends. But our task is to discover who God is leading to support our ministry, and then let the donor define the relationship.

6. They support other ministries, showing that giving is a way of life for them.

> *I was sure that since Lance was a heavy giver to one cause, he would not give to our work. But he said he also gave to two other groups in town and wanted to hear about ours too.* (campus staff member in a small college town)

Sixty-nine percent of Americans give to charities, and most of them give to more than one cause. In 1996 an amazing two-thirds of all charitable giving to nonreligious causes came from church members who also gave to their church. "Christians are the backbone of virtually all charitable causes in America. They give most of the money and do a great deal of the work."[6] A donor to an overseas ministry will consider adding a commitment to a local youth outreach. A donor to high-school work will consider a gift to make an impact on the university. A person who cares about your cause will often give to more than one project or person within your agency, if he knows the need.

> *We were surprised that Lance gave at a certain level or not at all. When we started out on staff, we'd settle for $20 a month from a large group of people. We learned instead that each donor has a giving level that makes them feel involved, be it $30 or $100 a month, $1,000 a year or whatever. Lance either gives at his "feel involved" level or not at all.*

7. They are asked in person and shown how to help.

> *I told our story with passion. He asked great questions, and I sensed good rapport. I told him we needed his help. He looked at me. I looked back. Well? I thought. I ended the awkward silence with a "Thank you for your time" and went away empty-handed.* (rookie missionary)

Andy Hartwell, director of the fledgling Bayshore Christian Ministries, flew to Arizona to solicit an older friend from his home church.

After two hours, he asked for a $50-a-month commitment. "I'm glad you finally asked me," his friend said. "I wasn't going to offer it to you. You need to take to heart, 'You have not because you ask not.' "

People don't automatically know what we want. When they do catch on, they want us to be plain. What's the best way to ask them? Among whites and African-Americans, the answer is a subject, a verb and an object. What if your prospect is Asian-American?

In the Asian-American context, it is best to do things with more deference. One Chinese-American staff worker with InterVarsity tells her story:

I put the needs in writing in my letter to an older businessperson from our church. I asked for a time to meet to discuss the ministry, knowing such people usually don't say yes the first time. I waited another two weeks then phoned. "Have you read the piece I sent?" "Yes, I did." "Do you have any questions?" (Not "Will you please support our work?") "Can we meet to discuss it?" "Not now." After two more weeks, I called again: "This is Irene. Can we meet to talk about InterVarsity?" "Yes. Let's get together." At the end of the appointment, he said, "I'll pledge $50 a month." A month later, he gave a one-time gift of $1,000. The process took four months. Going faster would have shown disrespect. It took time, but now he's a real team member.

Asian-American involvement is rising quickly in nonprofits outside the local church. Still, in many Asian-American settings, your ministry won't be well-known. If possible, your pastor or an elder should do the asking for you. Each one of the many Asian-American churches has its own norms.

Involve your pastor and elders in deciding to join your mission. Let them see what you find so compelling that you would alter your career path. Arrange a meeting between a leader in the agency and your pastor or the relevant leader. Ask him if it is acceptable to approach individuals. Their blessing and help in forming a support team will make a great impact.

The odds are that your own agency does not offer specialized training for Asian-Americans, so find veteran Asian-Americans who model success. If you cannot find such a person in your agency, find someone in another organization. Seek his counsel and if possible go with him when he presents his own work somewhere.

8. The case for your ministry makes sense. What has God called your organization to do? Does it have a credible plan to reach its goal? What's being asked of the donor and why? Why are funds needed at this time? Who else endorses the work?

Values, making a difference, personal trust, a giving lifestyle and a no-pressure invitation all matter. But your donor needs a commitment in writing. Even if she likes you and wants to give, she may have to answer a skeptical spouse or fellow committee person. A good first appointment often ends with, "Do you have something written out that I can show our board?" In part two we'll show you how to construct such a "case statement" that conveys your vision and sets the needed elements in order.

WRAP

Bill Hautt of Focus Consultants sums it up: "As we connect with select people consistently over time, for the purpose of sharing the mission, and as we call these people to commitment based on the interests and abilities that God has given them, God will provide the funds for the vision he has given us. *Fund development is a relational process guided by a vision.*"[7]

We connect with people around a common vision. We invite them to join us in advancing that vision. When they see us as agents to accomplish a task that God has laid on their heart, we've found the partners we're looking for. FOCUS puts its insight into a framework for all fund development.

Case: What's the need, and what's our vision to meet it?
Leadership: Who has the highest ownership of the mission and would help find its donors?
Prospects: Who has the interest and ability to help the mission?
Strategy: Based on the interest and ability of our prospects, what is the best way to approach them?
Plan: What actions shall we take? Who does which task? When?

By listening to Scripture, examining ourselves and thinking about our potential donors, we've come to a relational philosophy of support raising.

Now we're ready to prepare with the tools presented in part two.

STUDY THREE: GOD THE PROVIDER—THE PSALMS

Psalm 23: The Lord Your Shepherd
☐ *List what the Lord, the shepherd, does for David.*
☐ *How have you seen him do this in your life so far?*
☐ *With this Psalm as a guide, what can you expect from God as you deal with the finances of your life as a missionary?*

Psalm 37: The Wicked, the Blameless and Financial Success
☐ *What does God direct us to do when we envy the success of unethical people?*
☐ *What financial promises does God make to the blameless or righteous?*
☐ *What does God command concerning worry?*

The Hebrew verb used in verse one for "do not fret" is literally "do not get heated." The King James Version captures this well with the reflexive verb "do not fret yourself." Our worry is self-inflicted. God's gift is a quiet spirit that trusts him to know and act.

Psalm 104: The Ruler of the Universe
☐ *What did God accomplish in creation (vv. 5-9)?*
☐ *What one great overriding thing does God do now in his creation (vv. 10-30)?*
☐ *As you consider your material need, how does it look in the light of the power and the care of the Creator revealed and celebrated here?*

Part Two
Preparing

In this section we translate the framework into five steps that come before asking people to join your support team.

Step One: Prepare the Case
Step Two: Find the People Who Care
Step Three: Approach Your Church
Step Four: Prioritize
Step Five: Organize

4

Step One:
Prepare
the Case

Why do you need a support team? Why do you need funds by a certain date? What's your agency trying to do? What impact has your agency made so far? Who endorses your work? What does overhead cover? What difference does it make for your program if you are fully funded? What do you say when your prospect says, "What do you want me to do for you?" Would you say, like Arthur in the *Monty Python and the Holy Grail* movie, "Any help you could give would be, uh, very, uh . . . helpful"?

People who *want* to give to you will ask these questions. When you answer them clearly, they have more confidence in your agency and you. People want to know if a ministry is really needed and how their gifts help others and advance a value in which they believe deeply. The purpose of a "case statement" is to equip you to answer these questions.

WHAT IS A CASE STATEMENT?

Building a support team starts with your vision for ministry, not with the need for money. The case statement is ninety percent about your vision and how you hope to carry it out and ten percent about dollars. It's what on earth you seek to do. Your organization may provide a basic case format, but you have to personalize it. You have to make the case for your piece of the overall mission.

Face-to-face presentations are the settings for using a case statement. It's there not just to give facts but to stimulate dialogue. Resist the temptation to mail it. Statements take a thousand forms: paper, video, digital format on a laptop computer. Usually it's several sheets of standard-size paper with big enough print that an older friend can see without a magnifying glass. It's there to help you invite support when you sit before a missions committee over a coffee table in a living room or in a restaurant. It is not a brochure for mailing but a piece to equip you for face-to-face meetings.

Don't include everything you know about your agency, just the highlights. Don't over-write it, especially if you're just out of college. Less is more. Go for substance, clarity and interest.

Good case statements are the fruit of hard work. When you don't do the preparation, it will show when you ask for a gift. It has to be so solid that it will transfer from you to your donor and from your donor to others. People will ask your family and friends what you're doing. Imagine them trying to describe your work.

COMPONENTS OF THE CASE

Theme
What is the most succinct phrase to summarize your mission statement? Start with a verb or gerund to bring out your niche. Give your donors and prospects a handle for knowing and remembering what you are all about. Examples:

Building a Future on a Foundation of Hope
(Bayshore Christian Ministries)
Changing the World—Right in Our Neighborhoods
(Center for Student Missions)

Your cover page of the case should illustrate the mission. A child being tutored, a person reading the Scriptures in their own language and an American teaching English in China all effectively symbolize a given mission.

Need

Why is your agency needed? Your mission is a solution—an answer. What's the problem?

One effective case statement starts on its front page, "When students you know go to college, what will they find?" and in smaller print at the bottom, "An introduction to InterVarsity-Los Angeles County." Then on page two, "At college, they are likely to encounter..." followed by bullet points: "critical choices about lifestyle, disregard for the Christian faith, racial distrust, relativism" and so on.

"What in God's name can we do about our cities?" leads another statement. The key problems are named with striking photos of kids studying, playing and singing with volunteers.

The need page must make a visual impact. A good photo that illustrates your mission field joins your text to give your prospect a feel for what you're trying to do.

A need page is designed to let you share *your own experience of the problem*. Tell a current story of an individual your program serves or your own story of being called to give several years of your own life to your mission.

To prepare for that moment, write out the story. Unless you do, you'll fall into generalities. For any story to work, it needs key details: not just "the mission trip was so great" but which episode you could not get out of your mind; not just a Bible study that changed your life but which passage and what question got to you and what you decided to do as a result.

Any story can be told in three versions: thirty-second, three-minute, or thirty-minute. In a typical setting where you are sharing your ministry, give a short version that leaves space for folks to ask you questions. Don't memorize your stories—it will flatten them. But rehearse so you don't ramble.

Mission Statement

The mission statement tells what your organization is doing about the need. It should come as a solution to the problem, take no more than twelve seconds to state and use no more than three verbs. Commit it to memory. You can riff about your experiences, but you've got to have this one down *cold*. It should have the feel of solid rock.

> *Our mission is to share the gospel of Jesus Christ by establishing disciples, developing leaders and meeting practical needs for education, employment, and advocacy.* (Bayshore Christian Ministries)

> *Our mission is to empower families to overcome extreme poverty through self-sufficiency.* (Village Enterprise Fund)

Values

If God uses you and your group to meet the need, what will be different about the people touched by the ministry? *Values* are marks that will stay with your clients for a lifetime. Here is an ideal place for a photograph of the people you're serving. Be ready to share two or three current stories that illustrate what your mission seeks to accomplish.

> *I got into Bible Club when a friend invited me. It has helped me grow closer to God and helped me to get friends into the High School Fellowship who didn't know about Jesus Christ. Club leaders are able to teach the Bible in a way that makes sense. Club also helped me build for my future by having a trip to visit colleges and find summer work.*

> *We seek to engage the campus through relational evangelism. Joe was a hard-core atheist until he made friends with Christians in his physics class. As they studied together, he came to see Christ as the source of their love and became a believer.*

Program or Strategy

Case statements too often simply list activities, for instance, "Bible studies . . . large group meetings . . . prayer meetings . . . conferences." Contrast this with "The heart of campus ministry is student-to-student witness," bullet-points of three or four programs and the support of a photo of two students in earnest conversation with an open Bible.

Future

If you were fully funded, what would you do in the coming three years with God's help? Bear in mind that people give to make a difference, to help improve life for people or to advance the values they hold.

A part-time campus staff member in upstate New York figured that if he were full time he would be able to train twenty more small group leaders in three years. The average small group in the chapter being seven, he could point to a deep impact on another two hundred-plus students if he raised his full support. That told his prospects why he needed their help and when he needed it. Along with the mission statement, memorize a single sentence answer to the statement: "If we were fully funded, we would be able to . . ."

The Budget Presentation: Two Alternatives

The goal of your budget page is to show what it really costs to meet the need. Lay it out in the form that helps your donor to understand the difference her gift will made. There are two approaches to presenting missionary budgets. The first is the "position budget" (not a personal budget). It shows what it costs to fund your position so that you can go forward and reach people.

On a position budget you put your expenses in one column and your team's or agency's in a second column. That shows people that you are part of an ongoing organization. Figure 4.1 offers an example.

A second way to present a budget is the "program budget." It spells out the cost of each effort or program you carry out and eliminates the entries for personnel and overhead. You and your agency should consider this format depending on how you work and whom you approach. Figure 4.2 shows the program budget for a high school ministry.

Sue Jones, Site Director
2001-2002 Annual Budget

	Position Budget	UrbanTeam Budget
Personnel Costs (Salary, Medical, Insurance)	$18,000	$370,000
Program Budget (Communication, Travel, Volunteer Costs)	7,000	140,000
Office Setup (Computer, Fax, Software, Rent)	5,000	31,000
Camps, Special Projects, Training Events	2,100	44,000
Training, Team Coordination	1,800	52,000
Overhead Expenses (Legal, Administrative, Accounting)	2,600	127,000
Total Expenses	$36,500	$764,000

Figure 4.1. Position budget

Sue Jones, Campus Director

	Homestead High	Bergen County
Volunteer Training	$ 2,000	$ 12,000
Back-to-School Outreach	3,000	15,000
Fall Retreat	9,000	45,000
Campus Club (Nine Months)	12,000	60,000
Contact Work	6,000	30,000
Summer Camping Outreach Program	3,000	15,000
Scholarship Fund	10,000	50,000
Office Rent	9,600	48,000
Adult Support Network	2,000	10,000
Communications	2,500	12,500
Total to Reach Our Kids	$59,100	$297,500

Figure 4.2. Program budget

Note that in this arrangement Sue has a position budget of $36,500 plus rent and scholarship line items. But the focus is on what Sue actually does. Her total budget is broken out according to how much time she will spend in which activity. Her salary, overhead, insurance and other needs are prorated into each category. If kids are to hear the gospel at Homestead High, this is the real cost of delivering the means.

The donor can give to the total need or fund a piece of the action. Choices are clearer here than in the position budget.

Both budgets are what we call "zero-based." In a zero-based budget, each donor is asked each year for help. Don't assume anyone is carrying over from the prior year even though most will. A request for renewed support is an excellent setup for asking for an increase or an additional project (e.g., if Sue needs a van).

Gift Plans

Every case statement has a gift plan so your donor can see how her gift makes a difference. Figure 4.3 shows a typical gift plan. List the number of gifts you need at each level, starting with the highest. Gifts are classically grouped in categories of leadership, major and sustaining. This helps you to convey your expectations without restricting your donor to a predecided figure. We'll explain how to present this in chapter eleven. Gift plan numbers should be based as much as possible on actual commitments you have so far and amounts (ranges) you will ask people to consider. For gifts of more than $100 a month put down annual totals ($1,500, $2,000, $2,500, $3,000, etc.). For monthly gifts of $100 or less display monthly gifts with annual totals.

Profile

Who is your audience? Write your statement with two or three top priority people in mind. The last page of the case is a profile page. Its purpose is to put your ministry in context. We recommend a photo of your team and you or your family. State how long your organization has been active and at what locations. Include your agency's doctrinal statement, names of board members, pastors, businesspersons, volunteers or other leadership types who endorse your ministry.

Avoid the trap of writing to your fellow staff or missionaries. Have a donor proofread it to make sure you're in touch.

Don't tinker endlessly with the case. State the facts, leave large

Leadership Gifts

Two gifts of $3,000 to $4,000 annually

Major Gifts

Annual	Monthly
Two gifts of $2,000 to $2,400	$160 to $200
Four gifts of $1,500 to $1,800	$120 to $150
Eight gifts of $900 to $1,200	$75 to $100
Eight gifts of $600 to $800	$50 to $70

Sustaining Gifts

Annual	Monthly
Four gifts of $480 to $500	$40 to $45
Six gifts of $300 to $360	$25 to $30
Ten gifts of $200 to $240	$15 to $20
Ten gifts of $100 to $120	$8 to $10

Figure 4.3. Gift plan for $35,000 budget

margins, go for a clean look and use photos. Don't spend a fortune on costly publishing programs. One mission in Silicon Valley currently raises over $300,000 with the aid of a $60 "works" software program. Go for excellence in answering the big questions.

THE MINORITY CONTEXT: GET THE BLESSING

When you have a minority background and work with minority youth, you are asking for permission to influence the community. People will assume you have life experience but wonder if you have the training. On your profile page, show what you bring to the task: list your schools, degrees, relevant honors or awards, and work and volunteer history that show you can make a contribution.

Just as vital, ask your agency to help you get endorsements from pastors, educators, parents and other community leaders. When possible, get permission to put their pictures in your case statement. If you are African-American, work through your own pastor to seek the endorsement of your local ministerial association. Don't worry about the amount of their financial giving; you are going to take that key statement to give you credibility with people of means both inside and outside your community. If you are Latino, the counterpart to the Black Ministerial Association is sometimes called "The Latino Pastoral Action Center."

If you are white, you won't be asking minority churches for financial support since you have other networks. But the endorsements of local leaders are critical since you are asking for the freedom to influence the community. Be aware that a minority community has seen a long parade of would-be helpers who have come and gone.

If you're Asian-American, you know that the blessing of the leaders in your community is essential. Your case statement should quote two or three elders who believe in what you are doing. If your work is among minority youth of a different ethnicity, endorsements from that community for you or your agency will be needed to open the doors.

WRAP

The case statement defines the need for your work and shares your approach and how to help. It is a tool to assist you in face-to-face meetings, not a mailer. Hard work in creating a case statement will pay off at every step on the way to building a support team. When you get stuck, stop and pray for guidance. You're translating a story from the Spirit and your heart to your audience, and the fear of the Lord is the beginning of wisdom.

Who should hear that story first?

STUDY FOUR: GOD THE PROVIDER—THE NEW TESTAMENT

Matthew 6:19-33: Give Us This Day Our Daily Bread
☐ *Where are the themes of worry and creation in these words of Jesus?*

☐ *How much does God know about your financial situation? What do loving dads and moms like to do when they know their kids need something?*
☐ *How do you think God wants you to live out "seek first the kingdom"?*

Philippians 4:4-20: Receiving from God Through People

☐ *What words here remind you of Matthew 6?*
☐ *What could Paul do as a prisoner about his material needs?*
☐ *What did others do for him?*
☐ *How did he feel about it and what response did he make?*
☐ *If this was your response to receiving gifts, what would change?*
☐ *Who is the source of wealth—God or the Philippian church?*
☐ *Substitute your own name for "your" in verse 19. What promise is God making to you today?*

5

Step Two:
Find the People
Who Care

Who cares about you and your story? In this chapter we'll outline a procedure to discover people who do.

THREE MISTAKES

Three common mistakes plague would-be fundraisers preparing their list. Mistake number one is to list only those who we think will give. Usually it's six to twelve people before we hit a mental wall. Our fallacy is thinking we can predict what God will move people to do. So replace "Who will give?" with the question, "Who would have any interest in knowing about me or this work?"

Mistake number two is to do this mentally rather than with pen or keyboard. You can see this when you try to recite the names of the people in your office or Sunday-school class. If you take pen to paper to physically *write* and *see* the list, you'll recall many more names. Unless you're Mozart, you can't do it all in your head.

Mistake number three is to build your lists alone. On this point, four heads are better than one. Open your notepad or computer and enter the names of a family member, a peer and a church leader with whom you can pray and brainstorm to build what is called the "segmented prospect list."

Don't be put off by the clinical term *prospect.* You'll find it elastic enough to include everyone from close companions to people you haven't met, and it's more efficient than "potential people who could be members of my support team," though that is just what the term means.

THREE CONNECTIONS

Why do people want to hear about you and your work? First, they may be people who care about you as a person—family, friends and your home church. Your particular agency may or may not grab them. *You* are the connection.

Second, your organization has a constituency of donors who give, volunteers who serve, a general mailing list and, above all, lives touched—along with their grateful relatives and friends. Ask your organization for an appropriate contact list of people.

The third connection is to that group of people who care about your cause. They may not know you and may not have heard of your agency, but they may be very grateful if someone tells them. How great it is when someone says, "I've been looking for a ministry like this."

To sum up, you have God-given connections to

□ people who care about you personally
□ people who care about your organization
□ people who care about your cause

Now open up your word processing or database program or get out the large yellow pad and prepare to write. It's up to you whether you retain this in electronic format or an old-fashioned, three-ring binder (there are still missionaries who raise over $100,000 a year without batteries or switches). Pull out your files, notebooks and any address lists or membership directories. Huddle with your other heads, one to one or together. The segmented prospect list (SPL) is the foundation for choosing donors. We'll address that in chapter seven. Observe it graphically in figure 5.1.

Figure 5.1. Foundation for choosing donors

Within the three connections, create a sheet or computer file (document for you Mac users) for each of the following segments. Again, resist the temptation to decide *for* people about their giving. The SPL is not a plan as much as it is a photograph, a static picture simply of where God put you in the human family. At this point don't bother to load information about phone, addresses, e-mail and so forth. Just enter the names in these categories.

People Who Care About You
- ☐ family
- ☐ friends of your family
- ☐ peer group members
- ☐ if married, people on your wedding invitation list
- ☐ people in churches where you have a contact
- ☐ members of the Sunday-school class you attend or attended

☐ older believers who have taken an interest in you
☐ former donors or pray-ers for any short-term project you've done
☐ members of committees on which you serve or served, Christian or secular

People Who Care About Your Organization

Ask your agency for information about the following groups:
☐ major donors
☐ former donors
☐ potential donors your agency wants you to contact
☐ board members
☐ former board members
☐ volunteers, especially in your assigned area
☐ former volunteers
☐ former employees
☐ people served—in the case of college ministry, alumni of your organization
☐ parents of current or former students in your organization
☐ event attendees—anyone who has attended camps, conferences, seminars, workshops, banquets, desserts, on-site visits, etc., hosted by your organization
☐ general mailing lists—scan them for any names you recognize, especially church or community leaders
☐ foundations or corporations with an interest in your assigned area
☐ your own agency—any special funds for your particular position or assignment or people assigned to raise such funds

People Who Care About Your Cause

☐ Christian professional societies (law, medicine, business, etc.)
☐ lay leaders in active churches, especially on missions committees
☐ donors to similar ministries
☐ former activists with similar causes (employees, board, volunteers)
☐ institutional leaders (for instance, college board of trustees, administrators, faculty who show evidence of Christian faith; government or

education administrators or personnel who relate to your area of work)
☐ civic groups, such as Rotary or Kiwanis

Hard the first time you try it, you'll find that reviewing and tweaking the lists two or three times a year is plenty. Your lists evolve with your ministry.

LEADERSHIP

In most of these networks, there is a man or woman with influence who could be an advocate for you. *They often possess two out of the three connections, deepening their interest.* It could be a respected aunt or uncle, pastor, church elder, businessperson or board member. Scan your lists with these questions in mind: Who could help me meet people or recommend my work? How have they helped other causes before? Through prayer and the counsel of wise friends, several names will stand out. Create a separate list for them. Some terms for this list are *bridge builders, core support team, advocates* or *champions.*

Urban Work
How do you build a prospect list if you are a city person, are not from a middle-class church and have few personal connections? Reverse the order and start with category three, *people who care about your cause.* Instead of going to your family and asking for personal support, get help from your agency to present the work to suburban churches. Let them know how they can help your work as tutors, mentors or in other volunteer roles (check chapter fifteen). Pass out sign-up sheets for your newsletter and volunteer needs.

Ethics
Building prospect lists must be done ethically. Well-meaning friends may suggest you take a moral holiday because they want you to succeed. Three ways I've seen missionaries cross the line are
☐ using the Christian Yellow Pages for contacts even though the directory forbids their use for fundraising

☐ calling through a church directory without the knowledge of the pastor or lay leaders

☐ swapping prospect lists with salespersons of insurance or pyramid selling strategies, betraying trust and becoming "unequally yoked"

If you cannot build a support team ethically, God does not want you to be a missionary. Let your conscience be captive to the Word of God.

WRAP

In building your segmented prospect list, avoid the three big mistakes: listing who might give instead of who might care, failing to write it out thoroughly and composing your lists alone.

Through your own networks, your agency's and your cause, God has linked you to people who care. The SPL is not a plan, but a photograph of those links. For each segment within those three broad categories, create your list. Do it creatively and ethically. Invite God's help in bringing to mind the people who care.

Your next step is to approach the key people on your lists. Begin in your local church. In the next chapter we'll offer two approaches, one for those who have strong local church connections and one for those who don't.

STUDY FIVE: SET APART—THE OLD TESTAMENT AND JESUS

Where does Scripture teach leaving the marketplace and depending on the gifts of God's people?

Numbers 18:21-31: The Levites

The Levites were one of Israel's original twelve tribes. God's law designated specific lands for each Israelite tribe, referred to as their "inheritance" from the Lord. The land would enable the creation of wealth. The Levites, however, were excluded from the division of land. Instead, they were set apart for the work of the priesthood. In contrast, Egyptian and Babylonian priests acquired large land holdings.

Aaron (Moses' brother) and his extended family were Levites. Aaron's family was set over the sanctuary and altar; the other Levites were charged with the care of the rest of the Tabernacle.

☐ *How were the Levites financed (vv. 21-24)?*

☐ *What obligation to give did the Levites have (vv. 21-25)?*

☐ *How does this text answer the idea, "Religious work is not real work. It's not right to live off the labor of others. We should each pay our own way"?*

Luke 8:1-3: Jesus and the Disciples

☐ *How were Jesus and his disciples funded?*

☐ *In verse 1, note the terms "kingdom" and "twelve." What parallel do you see with Numbers 18?*

☐ *How do these verses square with the comment, "Personal support is not biblical"?*

☐ *What do you think was the motive of the women?*

☐ *Compare Luke 10:1-12: Who was supposed to fund the mission of the seventy?*

☐ *What might this passage say to the concept of using your own funds to pay for your work?*

6

Step Three: Approach Your Church

The way to your ministry is through the local church. If you don't have a local church to call your home, you must find one. How long will that take? If you're really starting out cold, it will require perhaps a year of active work.

Does that sound discouraging? Consider three facts. One, you need a church for the same reasons we all do. Two, by laying a foundation at the start of your work, you avoid a constant struggle for funds. What's the point of launching out just to crash in six months because you're in debt? Take a longer view, and the extra months look reasonable. Three, you can be involved in a local church and still connect to your mission agency.

Dear Headquarters,

I came on staff as I moved to _____. When looking for a church, we considered their openness to our ministry as one factor. We joined the church and became very involved. After six months as members, I submitted a proposal to the council for support. I had been included on their offering list and received gifts. So I asked them to become my "sending" church. Specifically, I asked to be commissioned and to be given a specific pledge amount. I did not expect the answer I got. They decided to narrow their list so that each ministry could be supported more significantly, and my ministry was not a high enough "priority" to "make the cut." What do I do now?

In Christ, Amy

Dear Carrie,

Greetings in the name of the Lord. How is your summer unfolding? We know many folks in campus ministries are on the road during the summer, and we really don't need to hear back from you until then, but it would be nice to get your response sooner.

Our committee is beginning its budget deliberations, and we're looking at a major shift in our funding priorities. We're considering all those in our church who are working full time for the Lord. What would it take from our committee to help you get full support? Is there additional money you could use beyond that for your ministry—materials, scholarships, etc. Please let us know what your wildest dreams are this year in terms of finance. Also, do you know of anybody else from our church who is in full-time ministry?

In Christ, Jack Jackson, Missions Committee Chair

Carrie, above, attended her church in high school, came home on college breaks and keeps a regular stream of communication going. Her segmented prospect list is filled with names of long-term Christian friends of the family. Amy works just as hard as Carrie but became a Christian as a high-school senior, and her parents have no close Christian friends. Like James, the missionary to Russia we described in chapter three, it will take her a year of volunteering in the church. By the church's standards, she is still a newcomer. Volunteering for a year is no guarantee the church will fund her, but there's no other way to find out. She has to meet people and trust that the Lord will confirm her call to missions through their support.

In chapter twelve we'll go over how to ask a church board to join your support team. In this chapter we'll address how to get the opportunity.

Every church is unique, so we can only give you guidelines, not rules. As a missionary you need to use all the tools of understanding people and groups that you use in your work. Each church blends doctrine, resources, social class, ethnic heritage, structure, philosophy of ministry, personality, geography and style to create a living congregation.

Establishing a Base in a New Church

If you're starting out, first look for a church that builds your faith and encourages you in your missionary call. Look for marks of interest in your form of ministry. Don't bother calling thirty churches in the area. That approach may have worked in an earlier era, but today most churches receive hundreds of requests and have guidelines for granting funds. Start by choosing churches with three of the following four characteristics.

Predictors of Church Support

1. Your agency has a basis of faith in harmony with the church. Some nonwhite churches may not use the word *evangelical* but are Bible-believing churches.

2. You have an advocate among the leaders. Someone in leadership knows and cares about you.

3. Track record of giving to similar works. If you are on Campus Crusade staff, the church has a budget for causes like InterVarsity, Youth for Christ, Young Life, Navigators, etc.

4. Your work is of high interest to the church. For example, you work with at-risk youth in a nearby neighborhood for which the church has a burden.

Then there's an intangible factor: do you sense a welcome? When my wife and I came to the San Francisco area, we had to choose a church. One was evangelical but had little vision for our ministry. Another wanted us to teach weekly Sunday school "in exchange" for $50 monthly. Then one wise pastor said, "Since God called you to a specific ministry, you need to join a church where you are free to share your ministry and its needs."

Pray for a real partnership from the church or a circle of concerned people within a church. One church offers $1,200 to a missionary who must raise $40,000 but forbids him to share his work with any other church members. The church will play a role in funding the missionary but isn't a good choice for a home church, since he still needs to find ninety-seven percent of his support.

Baffling as the local church scene may be, you can find your niche. What follows is not a one-size-fits-all plan but a number of steps to help you get rooted in a local fellowship.

1. Attend worship. If you are in youth work, tying up evenings and weekends, you will miss some Sundays. Try some midweek or regular daytime meetings.

2. Attend a Christian education class. Get involved in a class with people your age or older.

3. Go on church retreats. These offer excellent chances for longer conversations and to gain a sense of the church's ministry.

4. Write a regular check. Give financially to the church, no matter how modest the gift.

5. Read all the church's literature. Read any statement of purpose or plans, the annual report and especially the missions budget. Is this church headed in a direction compatible with yours? Could your work be a solution to a problem they see? Do they give to causes similar to yours? What amounts do they give? What is the giving calendar of the church? What protocol do they seem to observe?

6. Make an appointment with the pastor. Ask him about himself, his call, his hopes for the church. Look for how your visions could benefit each other. For instance, he may want to develop an outreach to at-risk kids, which your agency is set up to do. Be open with him that you hope the church will help fund your work, and ask him how best to proceed. *Walk in the light.* After all, you are asking the Lord to show you where to plug in. If there is no welcome for your work here, you're both better off knowing that early, so you can move on.

Take your case statement and other literature from your agency. Make sure one of the pieces spells out your agency's statement of doctrine. If it's a multistaff church, you may not find it best to meet with the head pastor. Sometimes a missions pastor, associate or board member will be the most helpful.

7. Interview the leaders. Your church may call them elders, deacons, a board, a council or some other term. Sample questions include

☐ How did you become a committed Christian?

☐ Why did you choose this particular church?

☐ How did you come to this particular leadership role?

☐ What are your responsibilities?

☐ What involvement have you had with the missions program here?

☐ Are there missionaries or staff of organizations that you feel have done a particularly good job of partnering with the church?

☐ Have you ever had any contact with (your agency)?

☐ Would it be possible for you to join me for a personal visit to the campus/city/neighborhood to meet some of our people?

Using the questions from chapter three, learn if he or she has children who may have been on overseas, urban or campus projects.

8. Look for advocates or bridge builders. One pastor calls them "champions." Be sure to ask your agency if it has contact with any people in the church. As you share about yourself and your work, does the Lord seem to draw certain individuals to you?

When the Lord provides you with knowledgeable, interested people, involve them in building your plan. "Without counsel plans go wrong, but with many advisers they succeed"(Prov 15:22 NRSV).

9. Join a gender-based circle of fellowship. If you can find a men's or women's group, become a part of it. Often these groups are inter-church.

10. Volunteer for a limited role. Don't bog yourself down in a year-round committee somewhere unless that is where the pastor or leader wants you. Some missionaries can serve in summer programs where churches really need help because many regular members are on vacation. A Vacation Bible School ministry to kids may lead you to interested parents.

Use your gift—teaching, worship leading, planning, whatever it may be. Where does the pastor want your gift used? What does your "bridge builder" think? "A man's gift makes room for him, and brings him before great men" (Prov 18:16 RSV).

11. Recruit a church leader to hold a prayer meeting for your ministry. Bring one or two people from your ministry to share how folks can pray for them.

12. Seek to be commissioned to your ministry. Ask the pastor what's involved in commissioning if you join the church formally.

13. Arrange a field trip or onsite visit. Take key people to your ministry to visit a meeting or other activity. Introduce them to your agency's leaders and volunteers. If you are in high-school or college ministry, introduce them to a couple of your student leaders.

14. Translate what you do into a service to the church. If you are in urban work, offer to do a session on how your church can help kids or on what your agency has learned about racial reconciliation. If you're in college work, offer to do a "College Prep" seminar for high school seniors and their parents in winter or spring. Plan it with your advocates and someone from the pastoral staff rather than showing up with the finished brochure and a request to promote it in addition to all their other activities.

15. Build your prayer letter list. After even a few weeks you can invite several people to receive your regular newsletter. In several months it could be appropriate to ask them to look at your case statement and consider supporting your work.

Developing a new church home takes time. "The plans of the diligent lead surely to abundance, but everyone who is hasty comes only to want" (Prov 21:5 NRSV). No doubt you'll be much more creative as you listen to the Holy Spirit and the new friends you make in the church. But you can start here.

When you've worked at this several months, you should have several men and women willing to help you in making introductions. You'll know many people, have enhanced your segmented prospect list and be ready to lay out a strategy for asking.

Nurturing Support in Your Home Church
Don't assume that strong church roots guarantee financial support.

1. Ask for the counsel of your pastor before you apply to a mission agency. There may be one or two other people you should seek out as well. If they are part of the decision, your chances of enjoying their support is higher. If you are in another city working or in college, send them a steady flow of information about God's work in your life and the agency you're involved with.

There's always a risk that your leaders think you should go into a different ministry or none at all, but you have to take that risk. If they aren't supportive, try to find out why. God may speak through them. Maybe they see an issue in your life that should be faced before you go into paid ministry or think a different ministry would be a better fit for you. Perhaps they just need more information.

2. Seek out a leader who is excited about you and your cause and willing to guide you through the budget process. Here's the advocate or champion we've referred to. He or she will most likely not be the pastor. Meet one on one and ask for the help you need, including advice on how to best invite financial support.

3. Arrange a meeting between a leader from your agency and your pastor or champion. Equip your advocates with firsthand information if possible.

4. Form a small prayer group. Meet over at least a six-month period while you build your support team (see chapter two, exercise two).

5. Read all the relevant literature. Know what's in print that touches policies, procedures and budgets. You may have been in the church for years but never looked at it. Ask questions if anything is unclear.

6. Put handles on your ministry. Show people how they can help apart from giving money. It could be mailings, a computer, hospitality, tutors, drivers. Keep a list, and as people come to mind ask for their help (see chapter thirteen).

TWO MASTERS OR A BRIDGE?

When a pastor or leader likes you, he may offer you part-time work or an internship on the church staff. Such an offer can either be the answer to prayer you've waited for or could pose a dilemma for you. Expectations could be tough to meet: programs, meeting with kids, parents, budget committees. Ask you agency to help you define the boundaries. It may be wiser just to volunteer at church and get your income through part-time work at a Seven-Eleven or Kinko's.

Sometimes it works better in sequence. Dave and Shalini Pickett served five years near Goa, India. Dave was a musician in a high-school ministry first. Eighty percent of their support came from grateful parents of those high schoolers.

If your church is Asian-American and doesn't know your organization, a part-time ministry position can give you the needed title of "church staff." Do your best to limit the commitment to a year, for one day a week. Social expectations may double your "official" time, but that may give you the most natural place to start.

After a year dive into full-time support raising. The longer you stay in a part-time role, the less part-time it will be. Expectations for your help will only grow. Don't get caught in a permanent three-way split of part-time work, part-time support raising and part-time ministry. There is no painless, fear-free transition from marketplace to missions. *Concentration is always a condition for results.* In ninety days you will know if it's going to work. Review your options with your organization, commit your way to the Lord, then go for it.

WRAP

The way to your ministry is through a local church. If you have a church home, don't take it for granted. If you don't, seek the Lord's guidance, then give yourself a year to become a genuine part of it. You aren't being "mercenary" if you are up front about your purpose; walk in the light with its leaders and listen to their counsel.

In Acts 13:2 the Holy Spirit spoke to the leaders of the Antioch church, directing that two of their gifted members were to be set apart for missions. The Holy Spirit, not the church, called Barnabas and Paul. But the Antioch church was called to recognize, bless and send them. If the Lord is calling you, somewhere he has a church who will do the same for you and your work.

"Since God called you to a specific ministry, join a church where you are free to share your ministry and its needs." Be a servant to your church's leaders, and invite their partnership with you according to their interests and abilities.

STUDY SIX: SET APART—THE EARLY CHURCH

Acts 13:1-3: The Holy Spirit and the Local Church

□ *Who gave the command to set Barnabas and Saul (Paul) apart for their special work?*

□ *Under what circumstances did the church leaders hear the Holy Spirit?*

□ *What preceded the Spirit's call to Barnabas and Saul (Acts 11:19-30; 13:1)?*

□ *How does Acts 14:26-28 add to the meaning of being "set apart"?*

□ *According to Acts 15:35, what did Paul and Barnabas do when with their home church?*

□ *What does your church have the right to ask of you as a missionary candidate, according to this model?*

□ *What should you expect from your church's leaders?*

1 Corinthians 9:1-14: Paul and the Apostles

□ *Why did Paul choose not to receive gifts in Corinth?*

□ *How should Christian ministry normally be funded?*

□ *What Old Testament support does Paul refer to from Numbers and Deuteronomy?*

□ *According to 1 Corinthians 9:13-14, who is a "Levite" today? Do you fit that definition?*

□ *How does this teaching fit with the example of Jesus in Luke 8:1-3?*

> On a mission trip to Romania, we planned a Bible distribution. One mission leader in the United States warned us that if we gave Bibles free, people would take them and sell them on the street. "Charge even a little." Sounded wise. But the Romanian evangelist said, "Even the Christians suspect each other of financial motives. If I charge even a penny for a Bible, I will be accused and lose my credibility." We deferred to his judgment, since he lived with the consequences. Paul faced a similar climate in Corinth and Ephesus (compare vv. 15-19; Acts 19:24; 20:34).

1 Timothy 5:17-18: Paul Advises Timothy

God's strategy from Moses forward is to appoint certain believers with gifts of speaking and service and fund them through the giving of the rest of the believing community. Paul practiced "tentmaking" for strategic reasons at a few points in his ministry, but as we shall see in later studies, he asked for money too.

> In a South American river valley, a missionary family lived in poverty. They believed that asking was unbiblical. Their mission permitted them to report to donors but not to ask for funds. After they used up their savings, they ate three meals a day of oatmeal, a diet poorer than the Indians they sought to reach. What would you say to them?

Mission lore abounds with stories of miraculous provision. But other stories deserve a hearing too: of savings depleted, paychecks skipped or reduced, nonexistent insurance or retirement plans, marital stress and divorce. Consequences follow our philosophy of fundraising. The Bible says "give me neither poverty nor riches" (Prov 30:8 NRSV).

7

Step Four:
Prioritize

After completing your segmented prospect list, select people for the priority prospect list (PPL). Notice how this works in figure 7.1. We use the term *priority* because they are men and women who you could ask in the near future to join your support team.

Figure 7.1. Prioritizing donors

Who goes on a PPL is usually not a matter of divine revelation. It falls somewhere between prayerful guesswork and guidelines.

CHOOSING

The men and women on your lists differ by how much they care, what they give and how they want to be approached. In this chapter we will show you how to evaluate that and then choose whom you should approach first, second and third. But first let's deal with a sticky question: is it biblical to treat people differently according to their wealth?

When it comes to worship, the answer is clearly no (Jas 2:1-7). When it comes to mission, each person has a different place *according to their gift from God*. This *principle of selection* is the approach of good organizations. Jesus had many disciples; he chose twelve to be with him in a special relationship and had a favorite three within the twelve. Paul teaches leadership selection in 1 Timothy 3. Wealthy Christians have a call to give beyond the norm (1 Tim 6:17-19). Romans 12:7-8 designates a gift of giving for a select group of believers. In the New Testament, while everyone is to witness and tithe, some are singled out to preach or to give or otherwise to serve in extraordinary ways. You practice the principle of selection in your ministry when you choose people for various roles. What does the selection principle look like in building a support team? Does this mean you reorganize your social life just around giving? Not at all.

Most Fridays at 6:30 a.m. I meet with three men for prayer. Two give to our ministry at a moderate level, and one doesn't give at all. I would pray with them regardless of their giving. Our seven major donors are not in my prayer group. I see the donors three to four times each year. I see my prayer partners almost weekly.

I sent out my first prayer letter ignoring the principle of selection, hoping for each person to give the same thing. When I started to listen to God's people, they amazed me by their individuality, and a few gave far more than I believed possible.

"A few people do much, the many do little." This is often called the "80/20" rule—eighty percent of the funds come from twenty percent of the donors. The University of Indiana Center on Philanthropy works with thousands of nonprofits, secular and religious. They say it's normal that

10 percent of the donors give 60 percent of the dollars
20 percent of the donors give 20 percent of the dollars
70 percent of the donors give 20 percent of the dollars

If one hundred people give to your work, twenty to forty of them will give seventy to eighty percent of your total. Three or four will give twenty or thirty percent. While every donor matters, you should involve these special men and women much more deeply in your work. They are the key to reaching your budget goal. But how do you find them?

Assess Interest

We said earlier that the three main reasons for interest are a connection to you, your organization or your general area of mission work. Here are other possible indicators of interest:

☐ church leadership—deacon, elder, council, board, Sunday-school teacher, usher, choir, etc.

☐ known as a Christian in your community

☐ active in a Christian or secular service organization in your community

☐ missions involvement—committee, short-term, project, donor, board

☐ youth work involvement as an adult or young person

☐ receives news from your mission agency

☐ gave a gift (cash or other type) to your mission agency

☐ he or she or a family member was served by your agency

Assess Ability

While we can't know what people will give, we can guess based on some observations. Six indicators of ability are *vocation, lifestyle* (that is, neighborhood, vehicle, vacation choice), *social group, educational level, family ties* and *membership in clubs or on boards of profit or nonprofit groups.* Of these, vocation is the most relevant. Identify who among your prospects fit in the following groups.

Entrepreneur. Anyone who owns his or her own business. Business owners are more in control of funds but have financial peaks and valleys. Entrepreneurs are consultants, stockbrokers, real estate developers or brokers, small manufacturers, importers/exporters, CPAs, farmers, dentists or engineers who are partners in their own professional firms. These men and women have been called the financial "backbone of the church."

Salesperson. "Salespeople like to be sold," goes the saying, and they can be generous. Some will introduce friends to your work. Be aware, though, that sometimes in their enthusiasm, they overpromise.

Corporate officer or upper management. Such people have high incomes but many also have high consumption lifestyles, leaving less flexibility than you'd expect.

Professional. People in the hi-tech field, civil or mechanical engineering, medicine, finance or government. In education they would include veteran teachers or administrators.

Attorney. While lawyers have the reputation of taking a guarded approach to life and are slow to make financial commitments, when Christian attorneys understand your cause well, they can be generous.

The Average Millionaire?

You might be saying, "I don't know any wealthy people like this; how do you find them?" Consider a study of over 1,000 wealthy Americans. From 1989 to 1996 the number of millionaires rose from 1.3 million to 3.5 million, and the trend up is going full speed. Contrary to image, just a small minority lead "a life of leisure by the pool." In its report on the study, the *Wall Street Journal* on November 12, 1996, said the average millionaire

□ is a fifty-seven-year-old married man with three children
□ is self-employed in a practical business such as farming, pest control or paving contracting
□ works between forty-five and fifty-five hours a week

☐ has a median household income of $131,000

☐ has an average household net worth of $3.7 million

☐ owns a home currently valued at about $320,000

☐ is first-generation affluent

☐ drives an older model automobile and buys rather than leases

☐ attended public schools but is likely to send his children to private schools[1]

You or your parents probably know someone in this category. Your biggest donor may not be the BMW-driving executive with the corner suite in your city center. He may be selling acoustical tiles or printing business forms from a small warehouse in the light industrial district of your town. By the way, what jobs do the leaders in your local church hold? Doing your homework and working through the adults you already know may bring you some surprises.

PRIORITY LEVELS

Read the descriptions below and make your best guess to assign a number to each name on your segmented prospect list. Again, these categories don't tell us how we want to see people. They tell us how, when it comes to giving, *people see themselves.*

Number One

Ability. These are people (or groups) who have the ability to give $3,000 or more annually. They can either give substantially now, or you have reason to think that at some point they will make your mission a high priority. You can get an appointment with them, though you might have to plan a few weeks in advance. The first gift to your work may well be below $3,000. But such a person remains a Number One even though he or she may be giving only $500 a year.

Giving pattern. Number One prospects have several income sources. Beyond a paycheck there may be bonuses, stock options, real estate and other investment income. Some may have little flexibility until they complete a major sale or deal. Many of them use financial planners and plan most of their giving annually, so they give once or twice a year rather than supplying monthly support. They may be asked for year-end gifts in addition to an annual promise.

Contact mode. They should hear from you by phone or see you personally four times a year, supplemented by notes relating to their special concerns in your ministry. They are active people who may not read your letters.

Number Two
Ability. These people can give $500 to $2,500 annually. They represent a broad range of ability. They are serious givers and are probably giving to multiple causes.

Giving pattern. Usually Priority Number Two donors have more than one income source per household, but most of it comes from one or two regular paychecks. If married, they tend to spend from a budget and give quarterly or monthly.

Contact mode. For those giving $1,000 or more a year, the right way to contact them includes letters, phone calls and one to two appointments a year.

Number Three
Ability. Below $500 a year.

Giving pattern. Since most income arrives in the form of a monthly wage, giving is done accordingly. A $20 to $40 monthly gift pattern shows strong interest.

Contact mode. Invite their support face to face when you are first building your support team. In the future it will be adequate to report by letter, phone or small group meetings such as desserts. Many of these will be friends or family.

Number Four
Ability. These are people you don't know well, but you think they have potential to be Number One or Number Two level prospects.

Contact mode. You might know they have financial ability, but you need a friend to introduce you. Next to their name, write down the name of someone who supports your agency and knows them. Find out directly or indirectly the depth of interest in your mission.

Number Five

This category is for all prospects who are in a nonactive status for any and no reason. All folks on the segmented prospect list are Number Fives until we put their names on the contact plan (chapter eight). Over time you will move selected individuals from this list into your contact plan. For example, you may be part of a church adult class or some Christian fellowship group. As you participate you will have natural ways to make your ministry known. The names of all members of such a group should be in your segmented prospect list as Number Fives.

Number Six

These are people who can help us to contact others but have modest giving potential themselves. Add them to your bridge builder list.

BUILD THE PRIORITY PROSPECT LIST

Using the form in figure 7.2, list all your designated Number Ones, Number Twos and Number Threes from your segmented prospect list. Include all other income sources such as foundations, income from inside your organization and any current donors. The priority prospect list looks at your total resources in light of your total need. Make sure you know exactly what your agency expects you to raise. Use a spread-sheet program or copy this form and use a pencil.

After you list the names, make estimates of the high and low amounts the person might give, using your best sanctified guessing. Subtotal your Number Ones, Number Twos and Number Threes and then add for the grand total. That total should be anywhere from 120 percent to 150 percent of your total budget. If it's lower than that, let your supervisor know, but go forward. If you have to raise $35,000, and your list only shows a potential $20,000, go forward and raise the $20,000. As you pray and work your plan, you will meet more people. When you do what you can, the next steps become clear.

List all prospects by priority on these pages. Include current donors and all other income sources, including foundations, transfers and overhead.

Priority 1 ($3,000 annually)

> **Gift Plan for Priority 1 Prospects**
> Need _____ donors giving _____ per year
> Need _____ donors giving _____ per year

Name / Range of Donation Request
1. _____
2. _____
3. _____
4. _____ Subtotal: _____

Priority 2 ($500-3,000 annually)

> **Gift Plan for Priority 2 Prospects**
> Need _____ donors giving _____ per year
> Need _____ donors giving _____ per year
> Need _____ donors giving _____ per year
> Need _____ donors giving _____ per year

Name / Range of Donation Request
1. _____
2. _____
3. _____
4. _____
5. _____
6. _____
7. _____
8. _____
9. _____
10. _____
11. _____
12. _____
13. _____
14. _____
15. _____
16. _____
17. _____
18. _____
19. _____ Subtotal: _____

Priority 3 ($100-500 annually)

> **Gift Plan for Priority 3 Prospects**
> Need _____ donors giving _____ per year
> Need _____ donors giving _____ per year
> Need _____ donors giving _____ per year
> Need _____ donors giving _____ per year
> Need _____ donors giving _____ per year
> Need _____ donors giving _____ per year
> Need _____ donors giving _____ per year
> Need _____ donors giving _____ per year
> Need _____ donors giving _____ per year

Name / Range of Donation Request

1. _____
2. _____
3. _____
4. _____
5. _____
6. _____
7. _____
8. _____
9. _____
10. _____
11. _____
12. _____
13. _____
14. _____
15. _____
16. _____
17. _____
18. _____
19. _____
20. _____
21. _____
22. _____
23. _____
24. _____
25. _____
26. _____
27. _____
28. _____
29. _____ Subtotal: _____

Grand Total (130 percent of total budget): _____

Figure 7.2. Priority prospect worksheet

PROSPECT PORTRAITS

Completing a priority prospect list is hard work. You have personal ties to the names you're entering, and it's hard to be objective. To stand back a little and practice, take a look at these fifteen composite profiles of donors. Where would you place them on a PPL? Remember that what we're trying to do here is be aware of how *donors* approach giving, rather than what we want them to do.

☐ Sue Krozak—39 years old, married, mother of two children, ages ten and seven. Works thirty hours a week as an accountant. Married to Tom, a public health consultant. Goes to Hawaii every two years; skis in Colorado. He drives a late model Audi; she drives a Suburban. She serves as church treasurer of a 300-member Covenant church and is an alumna of the campus where you are on staff. Tom worked his way through State College.

    Priority: 2

    Ask: $100-120/mo or $1,200-1,500/yr

☐ Uncle George—60 years old, stockbroker. Active in Kiwanis. He lives out of state, and you last saw him at Christmas during your junior year in college. Drives a late-model Cadillac and winters in Florida. Attends church two or three times a year. Divorced and remarried.

    Priority: 3

    Ask: $100 one-time

☐ Norm Pickett—26 years old, Radio Shack manager, alumnus of a campus ministry. Shares apartment with another guy. Active in local independent fellowship. Drives a 1997 Nissan Altima, lots of CDs.

    Priority: 2 or 3

    Ask: $25-50/mo or $300-600/yr

☐ Kate Gerst—48 years old, single, teacher. Long history of participation in Christian activities. Met you at a Sunday-school class on the topic "Science and Christianity."

    Priority: 2 or 3

    Ask: $40-60/mo or $480-720/yr

☐ Grace Lutheran—Pastor Pete Petersen, who went to Concordia College and Seminary. The church does not have a "missions" budget but does support denominational programs, including $1,000 a year to ecumenical campus ministries, a local food bank and a homeless shelter. Three hundred attending members.

Priority: 3

Ask: $500/yr for a city ministry

☐ Roger Chan—48 years old, married, four children. Senior Engineer at TechLabs, a midsize company. Elder in First Chinese Baptist, a city church eighteen miles from his home. Wife works part time and teaches Sunday school. Drives a late model Toyota wagon. A college daughter went on a summer mission to the people group you serve.

Priority: 2

Ask: $30-60/mo or $360-720/yr

☐ Jack Smartz—28 years old, programmer for Lucent Technologies. Ski racks on his new Saab. Single. Owns a tract home. Active in the Presbyterian singles group and a midweek Bible study. His study leader is a tutor to disadvantaged kids through your urban agency.

Priority: 2

Ask: $1,000-2,000/yr

☐ David and May Park—fifties, active in First Korean Methodist. He is an elder; she teaches in the children's school. They attend the English language service. He own several small businesses in the downtown area. His son is in your Bible study at Northwestern.

Priority: 2

Ask: $80-120/mo or $1,000-1,500/yr

☐ First Presbyterian Church—1,100 members. Has a missions budget that sends $4,000 a year to two staff of other youth ministries. Pastor Thomas is almost impossible to see and refers you to his elder for missions, Mrs. Smith. Most church kids attend college at secular universities. The church is five miles from the high school where you do outreach.

Priority: 1

Ask: $2,000-4,000/yr, but check first with Elder Smith

☐ Linda Richards—46 years old, married to Robert, real estate broker.

Has two teens and is active on the General Baptist Church Parent Committee. You met as a result of your serving on the staff of the church's Vacation Bible School, where you helped her child to have a deeper relationship with the Lord.

Priority: 2

Ask: $1,000-2,000/yr

☐ Wilson Anderson—49 years old, owner of the second largest Chevrolet dealership in your area. Family man. African American. Never uses alcohol or profanity. Active in his Baptist church and Elks and, once in a while, comes to Christians-in-Business, which meets monthly and is where you met. Wants to know who is on the local council of your youth ministry.

Priority: 2

Ask: $500/yr or $1,000 over two years

☐ Sally Leung—34 years old, single. Lawyer in a downtown firm. Active in church and small group Bible study. Active through her college days in a mostly white local church that had a college fellowship.

Priority: 2

Ask: $50-120/mo or $500-1,500/yr

☐ Frank Green—57 years old, married, 3 children. Owns a small company that does specialized business printing. Drives a older Buick; his wife has a sport utility vehicle. Lives in a nice two-story suburban home. Plays golf. Has been a deacon; regularly attends an Evangelical Free church. Shook your hand after you were introduced in the adult Sunday-school class.

Priority: 1? 2?

Ask: $500-1,000/yr

☐ Angela Garza—33 years old, married to Phil. No children, homeowner. Administrative assistant to a dean of the college where you minister. Angela is on the steering committee of a small group to start a new Bible class for her growing independent church.

Priority: 3

Ask: $20-40/mo or $240-480/yr

☐ Bill Rogers—36 years old, family man. Med-tech at Community

Hospital. Coaches Little League; drives a late Chevy. Mentions he was stationed in Norfolk with the Navy where he volunteered in a ministry to at-risk kids. You met him at a prayer meeting in your new church.

Priority: 3

Ask: $25-50/mo or $300-600/yr

WRAP

The priority prospect list is where it all starts to come together. Select the people from your segmented prospect list (SPL) that you're ready to ask. Start with the people with the strongest indications of interest and ability. List every source of possible giving. Estimate what they might give, both high and low, and total.

As with creating your SPL, get help from someone with experience, in or outside your agency. Evaluate half a dozen names together.

When you're going full-time at forming your support team, review and adjust the PPL each day. You have your case and your SPL; now you've prioritized. Next we'll show you have to keep track of data and manage the calendar.

STUDY SEVEN: ASKING FOR OTHER PEOPLE

2 Corinthians 8—9

The Jerusalem church had fallen into poverty stemming from famine. Paul had both a heart concern for the Christians there and a strategic concern for Christian unity (compare Rom 15:25-29). We don't have apostolic authority over donors, but we can follow the principles he models.

☐ *What had the Corinthians promised to do (8:3, 6-7, 10; compare 1 Cor 16:1-4)?*

☐ *Who was going to benefit (8:4)?*

☐ *How long had the promise been unfulfilled (8:10)?*

☐ *Who brought the letter that was read aloud to leaders or the whole church (8:16—9:3)?*

☐ *What was Paul's next step (9:4-5)?*

☐ *Paul already told the Philippians what the Corinthian church would do.*

What exactly did he say (9:2-5)?

☐ *In 8:10-12 Paul deals with an objection the Corinthians might have. What is the objection and Paul's answer to it?*

☐ *Paul holds out an incentive for giving in 9:6-11. What is it?*

☐ *In 9:12-14 Paul teaches a surpassing incentive for giving. What is that?*

☐ *What did Paul risk by writing to the Corinthian church about money in this way? Why was he so bold?*

☐ *If your support needs were met, who would benefit?*

☐ *How do you feel about putting your relationships on the line for the needs of God's people?*

☐ *How do you feel about putting your relationships on the line for those who have never heard the gospel?*

8

Step Five: Organize

Real missionaries aren't data managers. That's one reason why, when we block out a day for working on our support, we spend two-thirds of it just getting organized.

My organization sends me printouts of who gives to our ministry each month. I have them in a file . . . somewhere.

"Be sure to call me in three weeks when I'm back from my trip," he said. What the heck did I do with his business card?

Just how do you keep track of everything when ministry has you going night and day?

You need a tracking tool. In this chapter we'll show you one that doesn't cost $300. In fact, any word processing or works program will do. Here's how it works.

SECTIONS ONE AND TWO: SEGMENTED AND PRIORITY PROSPECT LISTS

First pull your records out of your file drawer, for the simple reason that file drawers are black holes for visually oriented folks, and place them in a big red three-ring binder. Put your segmented and priority prospect lists as section one and section two. Now boot up your computer and look at the form in figure 8.1, called the contact plan (CP) worksheet. A copy for each donor goes in the third section of your binder.

Consider three ways to keep your data handy: hard copy, a simple computer program and a more complex computer program. It's smart to have paper so you can keep moving when there's a brownout, a hard drive crash, or the oscillations of a third-world power supply. A simple software program is your standard "works" bundle with a database template. A more complex approach would be Microsoft Office's Access. (Use the "Contact Management" wizard by the way, not "Donations.")

SECTION THREE: THE CP WORKSHEET

You need a tool that easily shows you both the past and future. Here's a simple one. Add a photo and you're there. Under *Next Steps* you record what you will do next—letter, phone, visit or some service you promised.

Under *Date,* enter your deadline or planned-for contact. After your call or meeting, describe both *Results* and the *Next Steps* you will take as a result. By doing this you don't lose the content of your last conversation.

For each Number One and Number Two prospect create a contact plan in word processing or database form in your works or office application. For paper, in your three-ring binder place a set of monthly tab dividers in section three and make copies of figure 8.1.

Place the CP in the month in which you next intend to get in touch with that donor. For instance, imagine it's January 7, and you just thanked Shirley for her December gift. She agreed to a visit from you in March to update her on the work. Record the date of your call and its result

Name: _____

Priority: _____

Current Gift Level: _____

Target Gift Level: _____

photo

Spouse / Children: _____

Address:_____

Home Phone: _____ Work Phone: _____

E-mail: _____ Fax:_____

Church:_____

Church Roles:_____

Employer: _____

Job Title: _____

Referred by: _____

Ties to Mission Agency: _____

_____

Interests:_____

Date / Results / Next Steps

_____

_____

_____

_____

_____

_____

Figure 8.1. Contact plan worksheet

("yes"), and on the line below in the *Next Steps* area write "Call February 20 to set up the March appointment." Pop open your binder, take out Shirley's CP from the January section and put in the February section.

Now imagine that your next three weeks are packed. You come into February and see your Support Team Notebook on the shelf and have no idea what you are supposed to do this month. You pull it down, flip open to the February tab divider and see the contact plan for Shirley. *Voilà,* you know what to do. Shirley is convinced you are well-organized.

As the PPL indicates, there are probably only twenty donors (your Number Ones and Number Twos) that make the difference in meeting your budget. Space their CPs out over twelve months. After your first year of concentrated work, you won't need to call on more than five or six people in a given month. How much simpler the computer makes this. My screen looks like figure 8.2:

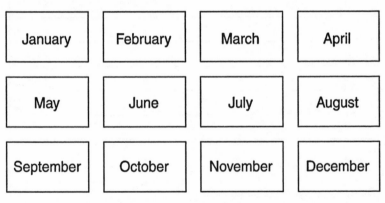

Figure 8.2. Contact plans organized by month

In each folder I have a word process or version of the contact plan worksheet for my Number One and Two prospects (current and hoped-for donors). When I have contacted Shirley in June and we agree to talk again in August, I click on her document and drag it from June to August. In August I click open the folder to see who I need to speak with. Lo and behold, there is Shirley and the other five donors I need to call or see.

When I open the folder, I see something like figure 8.3.

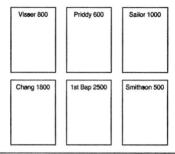

Figure 8.3. Monthly contact folder

I title each file with the prospect's last name and current gift level. I open it and know what to do next. After I see Shirley, I fill in the Results and Next Steps and then move the file to the folder of the next month I plan to call. Hard to believe, but this gives me as much flexibility as many expensive tracking programs in that (1) I don't need to find a record in one document and open another for planning and (2) the room for comments and important background information is infinite. A $99 scanner allows me to add photos easily.

Of course, hardware and software are advancing so rapidly that you've already thought of a better way.

Now our planning pyramid is complete as seen in figure 8.4.

Figure 8.4. Planning pyramid

SECTION FOUR: DONOR RECORDS

Each month or more often your agency should give you a donor report via snail mail or electronically. Keep it in section four. A good donor report includes

☐ name
☐ date when the gift was received
☐ amount of gift
☐ amount of last year's gift for the same month
☐ a running total for the fiscal year so far (year-to-date)
☐ a current address list of all people who gave in the month

SECTION FIVE: BUDGET AND EXPENSE RECORDS

How much do you need to raise? Your answer should always be crystal clear: "I need to raise (state full budget amount); of that, X amount is promised, so I'm working on the remaining Y."

Your agency support staff should print out a periodic report to show how far above or below budget your own ministry is. Each time you receive the report, take a moment to think out your current answer to the question.

Keep all the relevant paperwork in this part of your binder.

SECTION SIX: YOUR MOST RECENT CASE STATEMENT AND PRAYER LETTERS

Read your case and the last letter before you do call prospects or write the next one.

SECTION SEVEN: HARD COPY OF YOUR PRAYER LETTER ADDRESS LIST

Your address list should be on a simple database program for easy production of labels. Keep your own list and compare it for accuracy, once in a while, to your agency's. Keeping your own copy is prudent, especially if you are in a start-up nonprofit. Typically they are too lightly staffed to solve inevitable mailing problems.

WRAP

Put things back in their proper place, and you will find them when you want them. Keep information where you can reach it: two sets of files—electronic copy in the computer and paper in a three-ring binder. Organize it by the seven key tasks:

- ☐ Segmented Prospect List
- ☐ Priority Prospect List
- ☐ Contact Plans
- ☐ Donor Records
- ☐ Budget and Expense Records
- ☐ Recent Case Statement and Prayer Letters
- ☐ Prayer Letter Addresses

When you need help you'll know where to go and what to do. Review your contact plan section once a week during your first year and monthly in the future.

STUDY EIGHT: ASKING FOR MY MINISTRY

Romans 15:18-29: Asking for "My" Mission

Paul asked for money (2 Cor 8—9). But did he ever ask for "his own" support? Let's look at another example from his ministry.

- ☐ *Why did Paul want to visit Rome (vv. 23-24)? Did he plan to stay long?*
- ☐ *Consider the verb "assist." In the context of the culture, what was Paul asking for?*
- ☐ *Why did Paul want the assistance?*
- ☐ *Paul had never visited Rome, but he knew many Christians there. So what was his basis for requesting material help (vv. 15-22)?*
- ☐ *Can you state your mission as clearly as Paul did?*

1 Corinthians 16:5-9: Asking for Myself

- ☐ *Why did Paul want to visit Corinth?*

□ *What did Paul ask for? For what length of time?*
□ *This time, did Paul know what his exact mission would be?*

2 Corinthians 1:16

□ *What does "to have you send me on my way" mean materially?*
□ *From this and the above texts, how would you describe the way Paul asked for support?*
□ *What can you tell financial supporters when you don't know exactly what your assignment will be?*

When Paul was first preaching the gospel in Corinth, he was self-supporting. With the church established Paul approached them for funds on at least three occasions—1 Corinthians 16:1-4; 2 Corinthians 1:16; 2 Corinthians 8—9. We also see that he raised funds from other churches for both evangelism and relief—2 Corinthians 8:1; Romans 15:24. Paul boldly asked for money.

Part Three
Asking

This section describes the basic tools used to invite support of Christian causes. You'll learn how to

Send Your First Letter
Phone Your People
Meet People
Ask for Church Support
Recruit a Core Team
Address Special Issues Faced by Women

For my first two years on staff I was part time. I had a part-time job and gave myself completely to the ministry. If I had extra time, it went to fundraising. I don't know what I was thinking. In my heart I felt like it should work out, that God should take care of me. It went on like this for two years until I was bitter, burned out and cynical about the church and why it didn't give.

Then our ministry grew to the point that I could no longer staff it part time. God said to me clearly, "Your ministry is going to stagnate if you don't go full time, and it won't be my fault. You have to ask, and I will tell people whether to give or not." It was a fundamental shift in my thinking: I just have to ask.

So I made it a priority, and the funding came in. It was strange that, as I did that, the normal funding came in, but God also brought supernatural things. Things I always thought I deserved by doing ministry. His blessing poured out in the crazy money that you never expect, when we didn't even need it as much because I was finally asking. But it took a huge shift in my thinking.

After preparing we must ask. While some say asking means not having faith, we answer just the opposite: it takes faith to ask. As you think about asking methods, keep the perspective clear. Your goal is always to

---

form a group of people who will surround your ministry with prayer and resource it according to their interest and ability.

9

Send Your
First Letter

The key to raising the maximum amount of support is meeting face to face with your best prospects. The purpose of your first letter is to help you get the meeting. Before you call for an appointment, send a letter introducing yourself and your new ministry. Because this letter is unique, we've provided a separate chapter on how to do a regular prayer letter. Don't ask for money in the first letter. Ask for time to share your case.

Assemble your address list. Go through your segmented prospect list and get the address for each name. Good sources for addresses include

☐ church directories

☐ your parents' address files

☐ graduation invitation lists

☐ university alumni departments

☐ wedding invitation lists (if you are married)

☐ Sunday-school class lists

☐ address lists for any previous letters you've sent (mission trips, etc.)

Ask your agency to provide three or four of the best introductory letters in their files. Then ask your pastor or your "champion" if they would proofread your letter and send a short cover letter with it. The official endorsement of your church will legitimize your effort and open doors.

GET THROUGH THE CLUTTER

Last week an older donor of mine received seven pounds of mail in a single day, along with his three newspapers. Does your letter have a chance of being noticed? Consider this.

Help your reader see and open your letter. Researcher Siegfried Vogele of the Institute for Direct Marketing[1] reports that a reader usually

☐ *sees the mailing address, then looks quickly at the return address.* Stamp your return address but hand write each recipient address on your first letter.

☐ *spends an average of eleven seconds reviewing the contents before deciding to read more or discard the letter.* His or her eyes fix first on pictures and headlines, not the body of the letter.

☐ *reads "PS" first, not last.* While a PS in a prayer letter will come off as a gimmick, hand write one to two personal sentences at the bottom of your letter.

☐ *after reading the PS, reads emphasized points* (headlines, bullet points, boxes, color) in the middle of the letter before finally deciding to read it through.

PROFESSIONAL BUT PERSONAL

Place on the letter a photo of yourself, your agency's logo and the address, phone, fax and e-mail information for both yourself and the agency. Include a general brochure. That saves you the need to go into too much detail and makes the link to the mission clearer. Use your agency's stationery if possible.

Provide your readers with ample margins (minimum of 1.5 inches), space between paragraphs and two pages of text at the most, in a font size that can be read without a lighted magnifying glass.

Think of someone, for instance, a leader in your local church who is at least thirty-five years old, and write to him or her *as an individual.* So don't say "as many of you know." Use "I hope to talk with you," not "I hope to phone all of you." Personalize each of your introductory letters with a hand-written address and a line or two on the letter itself.

FOUR PARAGRAPHS

Briefly tell your reader what you have been and will be doing. For example, "I will soon graduate from Washington U. But this fall I won't be in engineering after all. I'm joining the Young Life staff to reach high-school kids for Jesus Christ."

Next, describe why you feel God directed you to the mission. "In 1997 I spent my summer with Center for Student Missions in Chicago. As I saw at-risk kids find new hope in Christ, I realized that this was what I really wanted to do. I may return to biology in the future, but I believe this is where God is sending me." A story from your case statement would go well here.

Third, summarize what you will be doing. "I've tucked a brochure about Frontiers in my letter. We will complete our training, raise our funds and then move to Alma-Ata, the capital of Kazakhstan, to begin our ministry."

For your white and African-American readers, ask directly for what you need. "Like the other workers in this mission, we need to find a team of men and women who will cover our ministry in prayer and fund it. I would like to meet with you personally for this purpose."

Consider a less direct approach for an Asian-American church setting. To your fellow church members, particularly those over forty, try, for instance: "The missions department is holding a potluck for me on April 12. I will share what I'll be doing and have information on how people can help. We hope you can attend. Call Sylvia at the office to RSVP." This removes the fear that you might ask people directly while still demonstrating how serious you are about the matter by dint of the hours spent and your pastor's endorsement letter. And of course, you still do all the one-to-one meetings. On those occasions let your prospect ask the questions. At the most let him know how to help but do not ask in a confrontative manner. We'll detail this more in chapter eleven.

When you approach most Latino and African-American donors ask boldly, but have a respected member of the community write the letter. This person can be a pastor, educator, elder or deacon, or even a parent.

In today's culturally shifting world, sending out two or even three letters may be important for your differing networks.

AFTER THE LETTER GOES OUT

Mail your letter one to three weeks ahead of your phone call. In contrast to advice you may get, we counsel you not to send a "business reply envelope" in this letter. Your reader may make out a $50 check when you could ask her for $500. However, if you've already sent such a letter, don't worry. Go forward and seek a personal meeting to share your case.

BAD TIMING

Don't send three hundred letters at the same time with the promise, "I will call you in the next two weeks." If you're working on it full time, send twenty letters a week, starting with your best prospects, and then phone.

If you're in your senior year of college, you may have no choice but to get that letter out and follow up after graduation. It's better to get the word out. Close with, "I hope to phone you personally after my graduation."

OUT OF REACH

The Navigator ministry wisely counsels staff to look at a map to see where their donors are clustered and urges their staff to visit every possible prospect. But there are always a few important people you can't see personally. Send them your letter; then phone and ask "Can I send you my ministry plan with its budget? I'd like to ask for your help after you've had the chance to see it." Agree on a time to call back and ask them for their help.

WRAP

Your first letter is to help you get face-to-face meetings. Ask the Lord's help throughout the task. Get good sample letters from your agency. Write to one or two key people and stick to the subject. Take the time to do drafts and get feedback. Let a draft sit overnight; then come back the next day and make changes. Get a cover letter from a leader endorsing what you're about to do.

Connect with your readers with a good photo and a personal sentence or two. Make it easy to grab the key points, and enclose a brochure that they can read for detail about your agency. End with a clear request. Tell them how to reach you by snail mail, e-mail and phone. Then with prayer and without fail, phone them for the meetings.

STUDY NINE: PARTNERSHIP IN THE GOSPEL

Philippians 1:1—2:1; 4:10-20: Asking and Thanking

☐ *In Philippians 1:5, 7; 2:1 and 4:14, the word* koinonia *is translated as "partnership," "participation," "share" and "fellowship." The word was drawn from the marketplace, as in a business partnership. What do these verses tell us about the nature of Paul's partnership with the church in Philippi?*

☐ *How is your partnership with your own donors similar?*

☐ *Since the Philippian church was "in partnership" with Paul for the purpose of his mission, what had happened to make it necessary for Paul to write them (1:12-14)?*

☐ *How does Paul assure them that, in fact, the partnership was working?*

☐ *In study eight we saw Paul making requests for specific occasions. How does that differ from the kind of giving described in 4:10-16?*

☐ *In 4:17, Paul says, "Not that I am looking for a gift, but I am looking for what may be credited to your account." In context, "what may be credited to (their) account" is their giving. The one who does the crediting is not Paul, of course, but God. This is explicit in verse 18 where he describes the latest gifts as "a fragrant offering, an acceptable sacrifice, pleasing to God." It's possible that Paul had asked the Philippians for help as he asked others. Christian leaders commonly ask people to help minister in many ways, not just because they "look for a gift" but because they know the spiritual growth that generous believers will experience when they give. The gift is a sign of the partnership between us and health in their walk with the Lord. In that sense we don't "look for the gift." We look for something far greater, partnership in the gospel.*

☐ *What guidance can you find in 4:10-19 for how to thank a donor?*

☐ *How can you deepen partnership with your donors?*

3 John 1-8: The Call to Support Missionaries

☐ *What were the "brothers" doing?*

☐ *Why were they worthy of financial support?*

☐ *What blessing is promised to those who support them?*

10

Phone Your People

Y ou wish you could just ask via a letter, but where is Rita P. (for Potential) Donor when she opens her mail? She comes in the door from a hectic workday and commute. A child needs her immediate attention. There is dinner to fix so she can get to her school volunteer meeting. She glances at each envelope to decide if she will open it at all and discards all that don't have a good claim on her attention. There are at least two other appeals from nonprofits.

Rita and her husband also take three newspapers, own four televisions, two VCRs, eleven radios and a computer with an on-line service. Each day they convey 853 ads to her. She thinks about forty of them and responds to an average 1.5. What does this bring her? A crushing sense of clutter with which she copes by a daily routine. This routine—a little exercise, the morning cup of coffee, the Today Show or Bible reading— are constants for her in an unsteady world.[1] You won't get through that clutter without a phone call.

DO I HAVE TO?

Phoning is the hard part. If people agree to meet with you, most of the time they will give. When you do hear "no," it's generally on the phone. Remember that what is in your mind ("I'm imposing and risking the relationship") is often far different from what's in your prospect's ("Why is she so aloof? Why doesn't she call like her letter said? She must be too busy for me").

The Key to Raising Maximum Support: Meeting Face to Face with Number One Priority Prospects

While you'll have to do most of this on your own, praying together and phoning with a colleague or supervisor is an effective way of moving past fear and getting the work done. Look again at the chapter on fears. Meet with the Lord first and ask him to remind you why you are doing this.

Basics

1. *Know your cultural context.* First we'll present an approach for using the direct, verbal styles which prevail in white and black contexts and then an alternative indirect approach more appropriate with many Asian-Americans.

2. *Call your best prospects first,* the people who most strongly meet the criteria of interest and ability.

3. *Monday and Tuesday evenings tend to be the best time to reach people at home.* Don't call a home after 9:15 p.m.; don't call a business on Monday morning, when all heck breaks loose. Call two to four weeks prior to when you wish to meet. You may have to call a businessperson or pastor several times. Have a reliable answering machine or service to take your calls.

4. After the small talk *ask directly for the appointment.* Suggest two times during the coming weeks when you could meet, noting you'd be happy to come wherever it's convenient.

5. Always keep in mind that the purpose of the phone call is to *set a time to meet.* Be sure not to start the meeting by accident with an elaborate explanation of your work.

6. Roughly half the people to whom you sent your letter will not have read it, so be prepared to *introduce the subject.*

7. *Always be up front* about the purpose of the meeting. Here are several ways to request an appointment.

Wording

Avoid jargon. Instead of the term "case statement," use descriptive terms such as "ministry plan," "mission plan" or "a description of our vision."

☐ *Hello, this is Tina Kuwabara. Is this a good time to talk? (Listen.) Did you receive my letter?* (Listen.) *I'm seeking to build a team of thirty* (whatever your plan calls for) *people who will surround this work with prayer and help to fund the outreach there. Could we meet to discuss it?*

☐ *Hello, this is Randy White. I want to follow up on our short conversation at First Baptist. XYZ mission has appointed me to go to Fresno. Now I am in the support-raising process for this ministry, and I'd like to meet with you to discuss it. Would that be possible?*

☐ *Hi, this is Scott Flannery. Did you receive my letter about my mission to Uzbekistan? (Listen.) Can you come to the dessert at the Hong's?* (Listen.) *I'll share about the work and the budget that goes with it. I'd also like to ask if we could meet. Would that be possible?*

☐ *Hi. This is Donna Duey. Did you have the chance to read my letter? (Listen.) I'd like the opportunity to tell you about the work and its finances. Could I have a half an hour to unpack that with you?*

Long-Distance Dialogue

If you can't set up a meeting, ask for a look at your case statement. Don't simply mail the case statement and expect your prospect to read it.

> *Hello, this is Ralph Davis. Is this a good time to talk? I'm calling from Lexington where we're doing our new staff orientation with XYZ mission. I'm now building a support team for it. I'd like to send my mission plan and budget to you. (Stop to listen.) After you've had a chance to look at it, I'd like to call you back and ask if you'd consider joining my support team.*

Ask Once

Remember the first time you led a Bible study or a business meeting? You asked a question and were met with silence. You got nervous and thought you'd been unclear, so you asked again in a different form—and again—and again, maybe until you answered your own question. At one seminar I heard a staff person say, without taking a breath:

Would you like to meet and hear about the ministry, to join our support team, but you don't have to, and I didn't think so, and I imagine you are giving a lot already, so how would it be if I call you back later?

At which point he hung up. Oops.

We assume the prospect didn't understand or like our question, but the poor guy only wants a moment to think about his reply. Like the kids in the Bible study, he's taking us seriously and pondering the request. Grant him the gift of space. Pop the question once and *stop*. Turn off mouth; turn on ears. You are about to receive vital information.

Practice your phone request with a friend or colleague until you can

- [ ] bring up the subject in the first minute
- [ ] ask once
- [ ] stop to listen
- [ ] hear an objection accurately and solve the problem it presents

Answer Objections

Most people on your priority prospect list will be glad to hear from you. Below are typical replies from people who eventually give. Most people who object are saying "Not now" rather than "Never."

1. Not now.

"This is not a good time, and it won't be possible to give now." "We just can't give anything now." "Our giving is maxed out." "Business is slow."

Response: "I understand. But I'd like to send you my reports for the coming year in case things change for you. Could I do that?"

Now those reports may not get read, but you've conveyed excitement about your ministry rather than anxiety about your need for money. Some people will respond once they have more information from you.

2. Let's have the meeting on the phone right now—the meeting before the meeting.

"What makes XYZ different than other missions in Houston? There are so many." "Tell me what's happening in the city." "How is XYZ run?" "Where does XYZ get its funds?" "What are you trying to accomplish?" and so forth.

Response: "I want to get into that, and that's really why I want to meet with you. Could we do that the week of _____?"

—or—

"That's a good question; to do justice to it, I'd need more time than I have right now. That's one reason I'd like to meet, if possible. Would you possibly have time _____ or _____ next week?"

3. What? Money?

"Is this meeting to raise money?"

Response: "Yes, but first of all we want to help people understand exactly what we're doing and why."

—or—

"No, not at this time. But I want to give you a look at what we're doing so that when we launch our work next fall, you'll be aware of how to help. I would be free to see you _____ or _____. Would one of those dates be possible?"

4. You're one among many good causes.

"I know a lot about Christian organizations and get a lot of information from XYZ. You don't need to take your time to meet with me. How much do you need? I'll send something in the mail."

Response: "Thanks for your willingness to help. But we have really put a lot of thought into presenting the ministry, and I would like to share the full story with you. I have a few days when I would be free to do that. Would you have a half-hour when I could come by?"

5. Way too busy.

"I'm not sure about my schedule." "I'm really swamped."

Response: "I understand. Can I call you in a couple of days when you've had a chance to check your schedule?" By the way, *don't* ask way-too-busy to call you.

6. How did you get my name?

"Who is this?" "Do I know you?"

Response: You should have mentioned the connection in your opening—for example, "Brian Grant suggested that I call you about my Habitat for Humanity work in Peru" or "This is Max Smith—Jane Jones introduced us at church yesterday." If you didn't or were unable to, state the connection.

7. No. I'm not interested.

"I don't want to waste your time, because I won't be giving." "I'm already fully committed financially to other causes."

Response: "Thanks for being direct with me. You know, though, Paul, you are a leader in our (church, community, campus, etc.). The bottom line for me is that I need friends who are informed about the XYZ ministry. Could I put you on my mailing list?"

—or—

"Thanks for your time, and I appreciate the candor."

8. You get the answering machine.

Response: "Hello, this is Dan Winters with XYZ mission. You can reach me at (123) 456-7890. I look forward to talking with you when possible."

Don't get into the substance of the call since you can't discuss it. In rare cases the prospect will return your call, but as a habit you should mark in your calendar when you'll try again. Make sure your own answering machine works so that you can be reached *easily* should the prospect try. Record a courteous, professional message. You're not in college anymore.

Since Each Person Is Unique

Pull out a contact plan worksheet and consider the person named on it. What's your connection with her? What seems like the most natural way for your to ask for an appointment? Before a call, write out how you will word your request and memorize it.

WHAT IT LOOKS LIKE: THREE EXAMPLES

Calling a Businessperson

Hello, this is Carla Smith of Center for Student Missions. Tom Beckett . . .

Oh yes, Tom told me about you. What can I do for you?

Well, Tom may have mentioned our plan. We're seeking a team of thirty people in this area to pray for the Northside neighborhood and fund our work there. I'd like to meet with you to discuss it. Is that possible?

The next two weeks are packed.

We can plan it out if need be. How is next month, three weeks from now?

That depends. I've got some vendors in sometime that week. I just don't know.

When could I call you to be sure?

Hmm. How about calling me the week before? We should know then. Frankly, why don't you just tell me about it right now?

How about this: we've done a great deal of work on our plan, and I don't feel I can do it justice here. I would like to wait for when you have thirty to forty minutes so you can focus on it. I also want to ask you some questions about your impressions of the problems in the neighborhood.

OK, call me the week of the third.

Great. One final question—what time of the day do you prefer to meet?

Sometime after 1 p.m. Can you come to my office then?

Yes, that works well. Thanks for the time. I'll call you on the third.

Although Mr. Businessman spoke in a rushed manner, even interrupting her opener, Carla's persistence and flexibility helped her see that he was quite willing to meet for a discussion of the ministry.

Calling a Friend

Hi Rick, it's Ed.

Hey, what's up?

Rick, I'm going forward with my plan to join Teen Outreach. I'll probably be assigned to Jefferson High. Now I need to find a support team to pray and fund the work. I'd like to invite you to be part of it.

Sure. What's involved, giving money?

Yes, but I need to show you the big picture. I've got a layout of the whole ministry and its budget. Can I come over and show it to you?

Yeah, that would be fine.

How's Tuesday?

Thursday is better. Work is crazy right now.

About 7:30?

Make it 6:30, so we can get it done before the Bulls game.
Great, see you then.
See you.

Ed's open, direct style with a friend doesn't change just because he's going to be a missionary.

Handling the No

Hello, Dr. Larson, this is Ron Jackson of CityReach.
Hi Ron, what can I do for you?
Sam Brooks at church mentioned that you had contact with CityReach in the past and you might want to be involved again.
I tell you Ron, we are just maxed out with commitments right now. We won't be able to help you.
I understand. Even though you can't fund the work, I'd like you to know about what we're doing in case things change in the future.
Ron, honestly, I know your time is precious. You guys really work hard. Go after someone who's not so covered up with other things.
Okay, I hear you. But I'd like to keep in touch through our mailings and call you toward the end of the year.
Fine, but I'm not sure our situation will be any different.

Because Ron asks three ways, he knows that Dr. Larson should stay on the segmented prospect list for now. And even though he did not get a time to meet, he has demonstrated that he and his organization are committed to their task. And if Ron keeps it up, calling lots of people in Dr. Larson's network with enthusiasm and courtesy, he will put his mission on the map and may just get a hearing from Doc Larson after all.

CALLING MINORITY PROSPECTS

Asian, Latino and African-American prospects may prefer that you leave them in charge of asking why you called. It's more important to precede the call with a letter describing your ministry and its needs than with the white donor. While the white prospect wants you to "come clean" and bring up the subject in the first minute, a minority prospect may choose to talk socially for a time. If he's in a hurry, he'll let you know. Let him lead the conversation until he gives you permission to share your agenda. This may go on for sometime. Finally, when your prospect asks why you called, ask:

> *Have you had a chance to read the material I sent? Do you have any questions? Can we meet to discuss it?*

If your prospect says "Not now," call again in two weeks and try again. If he says yes, ask where and when would be best and thank him. It is always best to have face-to-face contact of some kind, no matter what the culture. The way in which you meet will vary. For instance, some Asian-American prospects will prefer a small group setting to the direct one-to-one preferred by white or black prospects. But all effective fundraising leads up to a high-touch, personal setting where the prospect has direct access to the cause's leader. Note: never use the phone to ask the older Asian-American prospect for money.

WRAP

Meet Face to Face with Best Prospects: The Key to Funding

Pray, review your knowledge of each individual and ask for the privilege of meeting. Commit your request wording to memory, and practice answering the basic objections. Be up front and positive about your cause. Ask once and listen. Record your friend's response on the contact plan worksheet. Then turn it over to the Lord.

11

Meet People

You've planned, phoned and been clear about why you're meeting, and your prospect has agreed to hear you out. You still feel nervous—that's normal. When your palms feel sweaty, keep a few things in mind: (1) This is God's work. He wants to advance his kingdom more than you do. (2) God knew what he was doing when he called you, so "Cast all your anxiety on him because he cares about you" (1 Pet 5:7). (3) Your prospect knew what she was doing when she agreed to hear about your work. She's looking for genuineness, not a slick presentation. Focus on your goal:

To form a group of people who will surround your ministry with prayer and resource it according to their interest and ability.

In this chapter we'll walk through how to share your story and invite commitment to your mission.

Prepare for the Meeting

Pray. Thank God for your ministry and for getting the appointment. Pull out that contact worksheet and think over what you know about her. Let's assume she is a leader in your church or the community and you don't know her that well. Make sure you can answer these questions:

☐ How did you get the appointment? Did anyone help?

☐ What did you learn about the person by trying to get the appointment?

☐ What do you most want the person to learn about your work?

☐ What are you going to ask for? Why that particular range?

☐ How will you phrase the request?

☐ What will you say if she says yes?

☐ What if she says no?

☐ What will you say if she stops you early and says, "What can I do for you?" or if she says, "I can't help you today."

Know your case. Commit your mission statement to memory. Make sure you have all your materials: case statement, agency brochure, a few response envelopes and an annual report, just in case. If you bring a video tape to show at the meeting, have it cued to the segment you want to show and make sure it's under three minutes. If she wants to see more, she'll let you know.

Confirm the time and place of a breakfast appointment the day before. Pancakes are small consolation for that lost sleep. If it's a lunch or evening appointment, confirm in the morning.

Finally, if you've never been to the location before, take a map and a phone number of how to reach your prospect in case of a problem. Great meetings have dissolved in Los Angeles traffic jams and Georgia back roads.

With your preparation complete, think over how you can be a good listener in the meeting. Relax. God's in charge.

Conversation Sequence

Telling your story is the exciting part of a meeting. What's scary is how to start and finish. Here are some tips. We've sequenced them, but there's no perfect order. Let your prospect lead the dance. The principle is that you answer questions that she's asking instead of letting your mouth go on autopilot because you're a bundle of nerves. Let's make the prospect a person missionaries are most uneasy about, a businessperson over age forty. He or she could be white, black or Latino. For many Asian-American prospects, the protocol will be a little different as we will explain after this script.

Step one: Know the donor. About half your appointment time should be spent right here. First, identify your common ground and the people or events that caused your paths to cross. Second, discover something about the person's history. For example, you could ask, "When did you become a believer?" if you know she is an active Christian. "Did you grow up in a Christian home?" "How did you choose your church?" "What are your involvements there?" "Did you have any contact with Christian groups in high school or college? (if yes) Which ones? Did you take any leadership roles in them?"

Ask questions about the person's work. "What drew you into this business?" "What responsibilities go with your job?" "Do you connect with other Christians in business?"

When it seems natural, use one or two questions to transition to why you are meeting. "Have you been active with other nonprofit causes in this city?" "What drew you in?" "What kinds of roles have you played?" "Is your spouse involved too?"

"What are your impressions about church life here in this city?" "Have you had any contact with the local campus/neighborhood?" "What are your impressions?" "Have you observed any Christians making an impact there?"

"What contact have you had with our agency?" "Would you be up for meeting one of the young people who's involved with us?" "Could you come over to campus/down to the neighborhood and look personally at our work?"

Before long your prospect will ask you about yourself or give you the opportunity to speak. Briefly recount when you met the Lord and share that three-minute version of how God drew you into your present work (see chapter four under the "Need" portion of the case statement). Tell your story to end with the line, "That's why our mission is . . ."

Your story should evoke a question or two about your work, but if it doesn't, just say, "Let me take a few minutes and share how we are addressing this challenge," and take out your case statement.

Step two: Tell the story. She'll fear that you're about to read her the story, so say, "I've prepared this for you to keep. Let me just highlight a couple of points." You'll know what to say next because of what she's said.

If you've already made the need for the mission plain, transition to the next step by turning to your program page with its photos of your clients and say, "This (young person or other client) involved with (your agency) illustrates our strategy for addressing the need." Give the three-minute version.

After some discussion state "Our goals for the coming year, if we are fully funded, are to . . ." and point out your top two or three. This shows your prospect how she can make a difference. She may ask, "Who else supports your organization?" If so, show her the profile page.

After any questions turn right to your budget page and say, "Here is what we need to carry out the work. Take a minute to look it over and let me know if you have any questions." Resist the urge to mind-read by offering questions such as "Let me explain our health insurance policy," or "I bet you wonder about the overhead charge." If your prospect wants that kind of analysis, she'll ask. Remember, if she were basically skeptical, she would not have agreed to meet with you. If you don't know the answer to a question, say so and offer to find out.

Step three: Ask. After you address the questions, state how close you are to your goal: "The total budget is $32,000. There is $14,000 committed so far, so I'm working on the remaining $18,000." Then turn to the gift plan page and say, "This shows the way different people and churches are helping."

When you ask, ask for a range on your gift plan. Don't pigeon-hole your prospect by asking for specific number. She probably has already decided what to give, and if you ask for something different, you'll undercut her ownership. On the other hand, don't leave her in the fog.

We hear requests such as "I need $17,000 in order to . . ." with no idea of what the missionary wants from us. Instead, point to a place on the gift plan and say, for example, "We are looking for thirty people who will cover this work in prayer and help fund it. To that end, could you give a gift in this range between now and the end of our fiscal year?" Choose your wording and memorize it.

And stop, as with your phone call, and listen. Your prospect will share important facts about why she can or cannot do what you ask. Your job is now to listen and note the problems and then work with her to solve them.

Step four: Solve the problem. People respond with four typical problems to such requests. They concern spouse, timing, scope of commitment and short-term financial difficulty.

My spouse and I decide these things. I'll get back to you.
    I understand. When can you let me know?

Note the date and make the call if you don't hear from your prospect by that time.

When do you need it?
    We're talking about our fiscal year. Some give monthly, quarterly, twice a year or all at once. What's best for you?
What else is involved in being on your support team?
    You'll get regular updates through our newsletter, I'll be in touch with you personally, and we'll hold two events this coming year where you'll be able to meet the people reached through our work. We also have volunteer needs . . .
I really can't help now. I'm not sure what our business will be like.
    I understand. Would next month be a good time to call you?

Be gentle but persistent until you agree on when to talk next. Then offer,

When could you come to the campus/neighborhood and get a closer look at what we're doing?

Stay engaged.

Step five: Handle yes—and no.

No, I admire what you are doing, but I've decided to give elsewhere.
 Thank you for your time. I'd like to stay in touch, however. You're a leader in our community, and it helps us if you're informed about our work. Can we put your name on our mailing list?

This turn-down is rare because busy people will usually let you know the bad news by phone. But sometimes this person will help you later.

Yes, I could do that.
 Great. Do you have a specific amount in mind?

Write down that number on the gift plan page and hand the case statement to your new donor. Then explain how to make out and send in a gift. Then ask, "What kind of contact do you like to have with the causes you support?" Take notes on her answer and *agree on when you will talk again.*

The Long Arm of the Law
You've noticed that we've avoided the use of the word *pledge*. That's due to the fact that in 1997 a new accounting procedure went into effect requiring that "pledges" be treated as "unconditional promises" and recorded in agency books as actual income. The trigger was a museum's lawsuit against a couple who promised a $5 million gift but changed their minds before giving it. This ruling overturned the understanding inherent in millions of nonprofit transactions, and now nonprofits in the United States must find other ways to ask. Your United States-based organization should delete the word *pledge* from its literature and substitute words like *intend, plan, hope, may, expect, if,* etc., in order to make the promise conditional. Imagine if we got all the government we pay for.

Step six: Follow through. Within twenty-four hours write a thank-you note mentioning the amount of the gift and when you will contact her again, for example, "I'm looking forward to talking with you again after the 7th." Record what you learned and the results of your meeting on the contact plan sheet. Good follow-through is unusual. If you are faithful about it, you will stand out.

Donors need to hear from their missionaries every six weeks. We'll show you how to handle that in part four.

MEETING WITH ASIAN-AMERICAN PROSPECTS

When meeting with an older Asian-American prospect, following the script above will be fine until you come to step three. Most white prospects prefer you to be direct, looking them in the eye and saying: "We are looking for thirty people who will cover this work in prayer and help fund it. To that end, could you give a gift in this range this year?"

Respect for the Asian-American prospect, however, takes a different form. First, it's always preferable if a peer can raise the question of support rather than you, leaving you to concentrate on describing your ministry. If you must make the request, show both budget and gift plan and then comment, "This shows the many difficult ways people and churches are helping." Your case statement should list a variety of ways to give—cash (annual, quarterly, monthly), stock, gifts-in-kind, volunteer roles, projects or scholarships. Depending on the individual, you may want to look back at your case statement, an attractive diversion. Look together at the material or do some paperwork. Don't stare at your prospect while he or she examines your proposal.

Your prospect will direct the conversation from here. He will ask all the relevant questions: Can you come back to me in a week? How do I make out a check? What exactly is involved in "taking part"? The questions continue until he is satisfied, and he decides when and how the conversation is over.

If you find yourself unsure of what the next step is, ask "What kind of communication would you like to have about this ministry?" Irrespective of his response, write a prompt thank-you note for his time and any other commitment he's made. Though your style may vary with the individual, there is no substitute for meeting personally with people.

SO HOW BAD CAN IT GET?

Perhaps you're still skeptical that people will really meet with you and say yes. Lest we think success rides on our beautiful presentation, consider this true story from a twenty-four-year-old appointee.

Sunday after church I had an appointment with Bill and Jane at Baker's Square. Jane and I both attend the women's Bible study. We all ordered BLTs. It's not something I ever make at home, and hey, anything with bacon tastes good. We were eating and talking. They asked good questions and were into campus ministry, so I was totally feeling the freedom to talk with passion. But all during lunch I was thinking, Boy, this is one salty BLT. My mouth is watering like crazy. *I kept drinking tons of water to get rid of the salty taste.*

Toward the end of our lunch, I pulled out the case statement so that I could ask them to join my support team. I looked down at the paper and there were little red speckles that were never there before. Hmm, what's that? Then I realized they were blood speckles. I asked Bill and Jane, "Is my nose bleeding?"

"No," they said.

I was panic-stricken as it hit me that the whole time my mouth had been bleeding. I excused myself to go to the bathroom to assess the damage. I looked in the mirror and was horrified. I looked like a vampire. Blood gushed between my upper front teeth. What a way to make a first impression. I shoved a paper towel against the roof of my mouth and gagged. I was in the bathroom for five minutes, and the bleeding would not stop. Other ladies gave me strange looks as I stood with the paper towel in my mouth on the verge of tears.

I went back to my table with my hand over my still-bleeding mouth and told Bill and Jane, "It's the strangest thing, but my mouth is still bleeding and it will not stop. I think I cut it on the toast from my BLT." (Yeah, there must be glass shards in toast to make a mouth bleed like that.)

They nodded and offered, "That can't taste good."

Nauseous, I sat through the rest of the appointment. Bill and Jane were still chatty and asked questions, which I had to answer, even though every time I opened my mouth they saw my horrible bloody teeth. What did I do to end it?

a. Chucked a reply envelope on the table and yelled, "Send money. Here's an envelope for your first gift."

b. I said, "Please don't mind my mouth. When I'm full-time and have medical benefits, I'll get this looked at." The guilt-trip method.

c. Used body language to say I needed to leave—looked at my watch, picked up my purse and shuffled toward the aisle.

I used (c), got into my car and sped home laughing, frustrated and asking God if that lesson in humiliation (not just humility) was really needed.

My sad story has a happy ending. Bill and Jane pledged $100/month. I will always remember that if God wants something to happen, he can do it even if we look bizarre.

WRAP

If your prospect agreed to meet with you, chances are high that she will give something to your work. Go into your appointment prayerful and prepared. Divide your time about equally between getting to know your prospect and sharing your story. Answer questions she asks and share your story from the heart.

When it's time to talk about joining your support team, tell your total and remaining need; guide your prospect without pigeon-holing or clouding the issue. Ask once and stop. Hear out any problems and work with her to solve them. Leave the case statement and other relevant materials with her. Then agree on when you'll talk again.

Follow up the meeting within a day with a thank-you note. Mention any amounts or agreements. Then thank the Lord for your new team member. And hold that BLT.

12

Ask for
Church Support

A sking for support from the church budget is a unique exercise and requires some special attention. Each church is special and has a different place in your strategy.

Not every church is a source of funds, especially a small urban church. Partnership there is not about money, but it's just as important because of the trust and connections they help you make in the community. You may be invited to preach and may receive an offering, but the goal is building trust. Don't go to them with a financial agenda.

That said, let's focus on your primary supporting church. By now you've got the principle down: you're building a support team through others, not on your own. Chapter six describes the real work of getting known and finding champions for your cause. Hopefully you have found one or two volunteer roles in the church, and people are starting to affirm your ministry. Your pastor or a respected leader has sent a cover letter with your first letter, officially blessing your efforts. Many of the people you phone and meet are connecting to you through the church. What's important to know about support from the church budget?

PROTOCOL

What's the asking process for your church? The only universal rule is that you never ask for funds on church property unless the pastor asks you to do so. In churches with a missions budget, there's often a sequence of a personal interview, a paper or electronic application, a presentation to a committee and a final interview. Even when the church is led by a very direct personality who makes most decisions, following the stated procedures is important.

Jim finished his presentation to the elder and the pastor. The elder said, "Thanks, Jim. We'll pass your request on to the committee." The pastor smiled and said, "I am the committee."

That's a great system until the head pastor moves to another church. Most often missions budgets are delegated to lay leaders. Let's look at each step they may ask of you.

Personal Interview
The formal process might start with a meeting between you and a missions pastor or lay leader. In larger churches the mission tasks can be broken up into smaller units of prayer groups, task forces or committees that connect with different kinds of missions. Find out who does the first official interview.

Application
Some support applications make getting into college look easy. Figure 12.1 is an example from a large missionary-sending congregation.

This church has more than its share of people who make plans for a living. Get out in front of the deadline of this kind of church because you'll probably need the help of a veteran from your agency and this church, who will need to give you feedback on your first draft (that's right—you're going to fill this out at least twice). You'll also need to give folks at mission headquarters time to find the supporting documents and get them to you.

Application for Support

This Application for Support is critical in developing our task force plans for the forthcoming year. The Mission Committee has decided that the receipt of completed forms is required before funds will be allocated in the annual budget.

Keep your answers brief (we know your time is precious), but if you feel that a more extended answer is required, you may attach a supplement to the questionnaire.

Please enclose a *statement of your ministry finances,* including your *annual family budget* (if we support you personally) and a listing of your *sources of support.*

Please provide a copy of your ministry's (or mission organization's) current *statement of faith.* A copy of your sending organization's latest *annual report* should be mailed to us as soon as it is available.

Please provide a list of your ministry's (or mission organization's) current *board of directors,* including all *advisory boards, giving names, primary affiliation* (congregation, company, etc.) and *location* (city, state, country). Please circle or enclose in parentheses names of those board members who are members of our church.

NAME OF MINISTRY: _____

NAME OF MISSIONARY/OFFICIAL: _____

NAMES OF SPOUSE AND CHILDREN: _____

ADDRESS OF MINISTRY:_____

TELEPHONE—OFFICE: _____

TELEPHONE—HOME: _____

FAX:_____

E-MAIL:_____

DESCRIPTION OF MINISTRY:_____

DIMENSIONS OF MINISTRY (GEOGRAPHIC SPREAD, SIZE OF OPERATION,

NUMBERS REACHED, FACILITIES, ETC., AS APPLICABLE):_____

MINISTRY GOALS: _____

KEY RESULTS OF LAST TWELVE MONTHS: _____

PRAYER NEEDS (CURRENT/LONGER TERM): _____

HOW WOULD YOU CHARACTERIZE YOUR MINISTRY ACCORDING TO THE

FOLLOWING AREAS (TIED TO OUR OUTREACH GOALS)? _____

—EVANGELISM: [__ %] _____

—NURTURE/DISCIPLESHIP: [__ %] _____

—SERVICE: [__ %] _____

—COMMENTS:_____

WHICH OF YOUR OBJECTIVES WERE NOT ACHIEVED LAST YEAR?_____

WHAT ARE YOUR PLANNED OBJECTIVES FOR THE COMING YEAR? _____

_____

ANY MAJOR CHANGE OF EMPHASIS FROM THE PAST YEAR? _____

_____

DESCRIBE YOUR MINISTRY'S GREATEST NEED(S) IN MEETING YOUR

PLANNED OBJECTIVES. _____

_____

HOW CAN THE CHURCH FAMILY BECOME MORE INVOLVED IN YOUR

MINISTRY, IN ADDITION TO FINANCIAL SUPPORT AND PRAYER (E.G.,

SHORT-TERM HELP, COMPUTER SUPPORT, PROJECTS)?_____

_____

HAS THERE BEEN ANY SIGNIFICANT CHANGE IN YOUR FINANCIAL SITU-

ATION DURING THE PAST YEAR (IMPROVEMENT, NEW SOURCES OF IN-

COME, DECREASE IN INCOME, NEWLY BUDGETED COSTS, ETC.)?_____

_____

IF YOUR MINISTRY IS OUTSIDE THE AREA, WHEN DO YOU NEXT PLAN

TO VISIT HERE?_____

PREPARED BY: _____

_____

Fig. 12.1. Application for support

Committee Presentation

After you've sent in the application, you may be invited to meet with a committee. It can be one, two or fifteen people. The meeting can happen over a meal, in a home or at night at the church campus. Missions committees are usually all lay men and women who volunteer. They rarely meet more than monthly, and agendas are usually long. My experience is that these people are the backbone of the church; they volunteer everywhere.

Prepare by phoning the chair or a committee member you know. Ask what amount of time you should take and where and when you should arrive. They may give you ten minutes; if so, prepare *seven* minutes worth of remarks and leave three for questions. Get there early, especially if you don't know the location well.

Apply the principle "Know your donor" and be mindful of distinctives of the church. Rick Langeloh of Menlo Park Presbyterian Church writes,

I spend a lot of time trying to convince some of our pastors that missionaries are effective cross-cultural communicators. Unfortunately, many seem to leave their receptor-oriented models of communication on their "fields" of service. I heard a missionary speaker at a Quaker church talk about the need to baptize converts quickly. That was the early service; there was no reference to it at the later service because someone reminded him that Friends churches spiritualize the sacraments/ordinances. Be aware of the procedures, find out what to call the pastor, ask if there is a concern they want you to address and, if you are unclear about anything, ask for clarification!

Missionaries should use their brains in the process. They should show how their ministry fits in with the church's mission policy and goals.

It is not always the flashiest, smoothest presenters which come off best to our committees. "Heart" has a lot to do with people's acceptance. I tell people they need to be themselves. You can't make people like you or support you. In the final analysis, if God calls you God will raise your support.[1]

With only seven minutes to speak, what can you say? First, thank the

committee for their time. Second, hand out copies of your case statement or other material with the comment, "This will let you see our
work in more depth." Third, take a minute to share what your mission
is all about: a few facts and figures, a map, how long the work has been
going on. Then share a story that illustrates the critical transaction for
which your mission exists.

It can be a crisis where someone was helped, a conversion, a growth
story, a church planted or strengthened, a new leader trained. Conclude
by sharing, "If we are fully funded, we hope to . . ." and state your dream
for the coming year or so.

Invite them to your agency's next event or offer to take them to see
the ministry personally. Then ask if they have any questions.

The Classic Trio
You'll meet three typical personalities on a missions committee. One
is the chairperson, the diplomat whose concern is to balance the
many causes and personalities on the committee. Second is your
champion, or the open heart who gives you eye contact and nods
approvingly. Third is the accountant with the poker face, whose job
it is to guard the budget. He is the one who will ask you to explain
your mission's overhead policy or why this or that item on your
budget is "so high." Don't mistake his businesslike manner for
negativity. It's his God-given personality.

Well, What About Overhead?
Overhead is what it costs to tie you to a larger organization and so allow
you to focus on your particular task. Organizations define overhead in very
different ways. Some don't include their office buildings, training or super-
visory costs; others do. *Never compare your agency to another,* for instance,
"We have lower overhead than ministry X." If you can't answer a question,
say, "I don't know, but I can find out." Don't go beyond what you know or
drift into the role of speaking for your whole organization. Your theme
should be excitement about your own ministry.

If the tone is hostile, don't get defensive. Say, "Let me see if I really understand what you're asking." You could write down the question and read it back with the comment, "Have I heard you accurately?" Sometimes the real agenda is just to be heard, not reorganize your agency.

Do your homework so that you can state that your group is audited annually and that it is a member of the Evangelical Council on Financial Accountability (ECFA). If for some reason your group is not in the ECFA, ask your agency how they'd prefer you to explain why that's the case.

Be upbeat about how your agency's services free you for ministry. "I'm sure glad I don't have to handle payroll, taxes, insurance and legal procedures. We're blessed that people serve us that way so we are freed to share the gospel."

Closing

After two questions from the committee, check your watch and look to the chair with a comment, "I think I've used my time." He'll let you know if that's true. Sometimes they'll want to keep you there longer. If so, take the initiative and ask the committee, "What do you hope for from the missionaries you support?"

Close the meeting by thanking the committee for the opportunity and asking them what your next step is. You may hear "We'll get back to you." Ask, "Would that be possible in the next thirty days?" Don't box them in, but let them know you need an answer.

Follow Through

Call your champion the next day and ask how he saw the meeting and if he has any advice on your next step. Write up the results and your follow-up plans in your Contact Plan tracker. Send a note of thanks to the chair.

While acquiring church support is often more formal than with individual donors, the principles are the same. For follow-through there is little difference. Every six weeks the two or three key people on your missions committee need a prayer letter, a call or some kind of contact with you.

A LEGEND IN OUR OWN MIND

We missionaries are prone to an occupational illness that hurts church partnership. Langeloh uses Tim Stafford's "The Noble People Theorem"[2] to analyze it.

> The "Noble People Theorem" is quite simple—"When one noble person meets another, they are bound to dislike each other." As missionaries, it is easy to think of the noble sacrifices. You didn't become a scientist, lawyer or doctor; you drive an old Nissan and not a new Mercedes. You work long hours and do the greatest possible thing in the world—you introduce people to God.
>
> Someday you may encounter a noble person at church. It may be a pastor who gives up his/her pulpit so that you can speak. That may be noble because he knows the love offering will bring the church's finances close to the red line; or because he's getting flack for not preaching enough—too many guest speakers. Or it may be a missions committee member who gave up his only night at home this week to hear your presentation. Or the woman whose husband can't understand her church activities.
>
> If both sides ask to be acknowledged for their nobility, neither side will go away happy. "The dual nobilities form a barrier between us." That barrier is pride.
>
> The answer, of course, is humility. It is servanthood. It is not our natural reaction; it takes a work of grace.
>
> What does a church expect of its missionaries? It expects grace, honesty and accountability. In short, it expects you to be a partner. It wants to share in your ministry, much as Paul described his relationship with the Philippian church when he wrote of their participation in the gospel and of sharing their affliction. Partnership takes work, but it's what is needed; it is what is demanded if together we are to help fulfill the Great Commission.[3]

WRAP

Getting your church's support is the most important step in forming your support team. Through the process you will meet people, demonstrate some of your gifts and share your work.

With the help of your advocate in the church, do your homework for the application process. Ask your supervisor to proofread your work.

Learn what your church expects of you. Get to know the people who make the decisions about missionary funding. Be responsive to their requests for information. Ask them each year for feedback on the partnership between your agency and the church. Seek their prayers, counsel and volunteer help. In other words, treat them as partners.

13

Recruit a Core Team

So far we've concentrated on what you as a lone missionary can do: drawing up lists, getting organized and asking for support. Now let's look again at the basic concept.

Form a group of people who will surround your ministry with prayer and resource it according to their interest and ability.

CORE TEAM

Forming that team is a relational process that can take at least fifty percent of your time in your first year of ministry. The good news is that with that base built, it can quickly recede to ten or fifteen percent. This dramatic improvement happens as a result of recruiting a *core support team* among your many prospects. Core support team people share your work. Sometimes they work closely together as a formal group with a name like council, friends, advisory committee or local board. In other cases they are networked to you personally and may even live in different cities.

Humanly speaking, the buck starts and stops with you. But as your group forms and you get to know them, you'll see how can work *with* them and *through* them to reach your goal. You need their help.

Gifts Differing

What do you need in a core support team? We've discussed your need for a supportive pastor and "champion" in a local church. We all want volunteer fundraisers, of course, but God gives us people with a mix of gifts instead: wisdom, service, prayer, hospitality, giving (cash and in-kind) and maybe even exhortation. And we need them all.

If you're headed overseas, you need someone to help with communications, to take your letter, get it formatted, stuffed, addressed and sent here in your home country. You need people with the gift of hospitality in cities where your donors may be grouped, prayer warriors and perhaps someone with the time and knowledge to assist with getting visas. If you're building support in or near your place of ministry, you too need a prayer group, a communications assistant, hosts for events to promote your work or encourage your donors. You need an advisory group, formal or informal, beyond your organization. Youth ministries need contact people for alumni of their programs. Make a chart like the one in figure 13.1 for all the roles that your ministry could use.

Prayer Team Leader:
Church/Champion:
Dessert Host:
Phone-a-thon Leader:
Newsletter Coordinator:
Computer Service Provider:

Figure 13.1. Volunteer roles

Next, look through the contact plan information and ask yourself why your donors give. How did they answer your question "What kind of relationship do you want with the causes you support?" Are they aware of the different needs of your ministry? What gifts do they have to offer? Let's consider five different ministries you should delegate. You'll think of more. As you look at the tasks, enter names from your lists of people who might be willing and able to help.

1. Prayer

Group prayer is a gift of God. In chapter two on fears we mentioned it as one of the "faith exercises." We have an enemy who does not want us to make use of the means of grace. He would rather deal with us alone. Take the promise of Christ in Matthew 18:19 and form that group.

Prayer walks are a wonderful ministry for a prayer group. Some ministries invite people for a "Jericho walk" in their neighborhood or campus, asking for God's presence and power to grace their work in that place, tearing down the wall of resistance to the Lord. Take a small group and pray at classrooms, cafeterias, residence halls, police stations, rec centers and projects, wherever God has (or should have) his people.

2. Introductions: Wrong and Right

Introductions—sometimes called referrals—are probably what we'd like the most from volunteers. Have realistic expectations. Most boards have no more than one or two motivated fundraising volunteers. A good volunteer will introduce your ministry to one new friend. A great volunteer will introduce it to five. That's fine because you want select individuals, not longer lists.

It does not help for your volunteer to give you a list of names, saying, "Call these people. I think they would be interested." They won't be. What you need is for your donor to invite his friend to meet you both for a meal. When Brian Wallace moved from North Carolina State to UT-Austin, a local real estate broker gave him a breakfast meeting each Tuesday morning for three months to introduce him to her Christian clients. That's what we mean by good introductions.

Gather the four or five people with the greatest concern for your work and have an open discussion of how together you can advance the mission. Describe why your work needs more donors and ask for their help to solve the problem. Your friends will tell you if they are up for it and how they prefer to proceed. If you are a local missionary or staff worker, ask the group to work together for four months; then evaluate and decide the next step together. Define the goal; for instance, ask them to look for folks who have the ability to give $500 a year or more. If you're going overseas, ask them to stick with you for your first term of service. They'll appreciate not being asked to do all the analysis or to be part of a project that goes on forever.

3. Events: Small Is Beautiful

We have nothing against banquets. With enough volunteers, paid staff and preparation, they have an important place in an agency's total strategy. You probably don't have that infrastructure, so what do you do? Gathering people from your own network for breakfasts, teas, small dinners, desserts or prayer meetings can also be powerful.

In such personal events you team with a donor to reach out more widely. If nothing else, you are building a relationship with that person. You will get major education on your donor and community through the attempt. You will increase your contacts. Even a poorly attended event gives your work visibility and creates opportunities to talk about it.

Local Motion

A donor couple in our city opened their living room on a Sunday evening for a dessert presentation. Our invitation was clear that we would invite financial support. We invited sixty people, mostly couples, and seven came.

Maria shared how she met the Lord through InterVarsity at New Mexico State, a student gave his testimony, and I shared our goals and invited support. Five friends joined our support team and met our budget. We'd worn ourselves down doing fancier events that weren't as productive. The key was letting the Lord choose the people and then ministering to those who came, not to those who didn't.

Out-of-towners

Here's the report of a missionary couple whose calendar was less flexible than ours. Whereas we were local, their visit was a special occasion. To deal with the problem of being in town only a short time, they found three hosts to sponsor three teas in a single weekend.

> *I provided the three hosts with all the people in the area that I had contact with and asked them for any people that they thought I had overlooked or that might be interested in meeting me and finding out about the ministry.*
>
> *We then divided the list, and two of the hosts invited their people, and I designed invitations for the third tea and sent them on behalf of the host. Everyone invited knew that the purpose was for me to share the ministry and provide an opportunity for them to become partners with us. I shared, showed slides, took questions and then the host led or opened a time of prayer, and everyone was given a card and envelope to take home.*
>
> *My follow-up phone calls to this were, frankly, a bit tardy. But these teas helped me to get feedback, share and be very encouraged by people interested and enthusiastic about our ministry. We are very blessed to have people who love us and pray for us regularly. I have been back twice to the Boston area and have seen supporters in church and talked about what God is doing.*

While less demanding than a banquet program, both host and missionary have to work to make the event a success. Since most hosts are women, we'll refer to the host as *she*.

Preparation

Agenda. Meet with your host and give her an idea of what you want to do in the program. If you want to show a video, is there a good TV-VCR system? If slides, who has a projector? Practice with your own slides, and make sure it works. How will media affect seating arrangements? Are there other setup needs? Who will start the meeting and introduce you? It should be your host, a pastor or another recognized leader who's coming.

Who will ask for the financial commitment and how? You can

certainly do it, but it can be more effective if an advocate does it for you. "We've decided to help support the Beckharts's work in Asia, and we hope you'll join us. If the Lord is leading you that way, here's how you can do that." Then your friend shows them how to fill out the card and send in the first gift. If questions arise, you can take them.

Have a time of prayer, closed by someone you've asked beforehand.

Materials. Prepare for the meeting with copies of any handouts, gift envelopes and response cards. Response cards run the gamut from a simple 3 x 5 to a preprinted card that has a place to indicate name, address, phone, gift amount, interest in prayer letter and interest in volunteering. Make sure your friend who asks for the commitment is familiar with all the materials.

Food. We suggest that your host designate someone other than herself to do all the work here so that she is free to greet guests as they arrive. Some provide the beverages and ask a friend to handle the food. Give them at least three days notice on how many people you expect.

Invitations. Build an invitation list with help from your host and friends of your ministry.

Content. The mailed invitation should include date, time, location, a map or directions, and an RSVP date. It should indicate if the event is a dinner party, potluck or dessert. State the purpose: "We're meeting to hear about the work of Paul and Lynn Leary with World Harvest Mission in Uganda and how we can help." Mail invitations at least three weeks in advance.

Phoning. Most people don't RSVP. The ideal is a small group of your friends who each phone their closest friends.

Phone your host three or four days before the event and then again twenty-four hours before to check logistics. This will reassure the host and allow you to catch problems that have come up.

Program
Show up half an hour early with a nice flower arrangement, plant or other gift for your host. Then ask how you can help in setup.

Presentations of local works shouldn't run much more than thirty-five minutes, leaving fifteen minutes for discussion. Overseas missionaries can take longer because people understand it as more of a special occasion. The meeting is usually over by 9 p.m. and definitely over by 9:15, unless it's electrifying. Leave the electrifying to the Holy Spirit and plan to end by 9:00. He blesses missionaries who end on time.

If you're presenting a local ministry, bring someone who's been touched by it and let them speak. Do what you can to prepare them, but authenticity covers a multitude of boo-boos. Try to set the person at ease if he is be going into a different social-cultural setting than he's used to.

State your case or what pieces of it are most appropriate. Make sure your friends get a clear idea of what you need, why and how they can help.

Donor Recognition

Some donors prefer anonymity. But while the Sermon on the Mount says we aren't to seek recognition for ourselves, the Bible is full of examples of believers recognizing the gifts of others (for example, Rom 16; Phil 4). We should never tell a third party what amount someone is giving unless they have some official responsibility for your agency's finances. But these events are fun times to express thanks for those who have helped in special ways.

No one expects a vacation for two to Hawaii. A special book, a plant, a plaque or a gift certificate to a favorite store or restaurant will do. A slide show with pictures of your volunteers at work is always a hit. It's fun not just to honor your fundraisers or chairpeople but also the quieter types who keep your used computers running and drive screaming junior highers to weekend camp. And of course, thank your host in the presence of the group, mentioning two or three tasks she did to make the occasion possible.

Follow Through

Thank your host again. It's Hallmark time. Let her know what a difference the event made for you and the work.

Contact each person who came. Thank them for their support or their interest in attending. If they did not fill out a response card, ask them for a commitment on the phone. "Would you be able to help us reach our goal?" Seek one-to-one meetings with the best prospects.

4. Group Phoning

All of your donors need a periodic phone call. Sure, they want to hear from you. But once a year it's effective to have a third-party call that focuses on the work, not just you personally. Even people who don't think of themselves as fundraisers can be a great help.

For instance, for supporters who *can* ask, a year-end phone-a-thon can be effective. Your agency may have a script for that, or you can adapt it from this book. For those who find that beyond their comfort zone, consider a *thank*-a-thon, where each supporter or prayer-letter-reader gets a call thanking them for their help, reporting on one or two highlights of the work and asking for one prayer request. Follow the guidelines in chapter ten.

5. Newsletters

Sue is a homemaker with grandchildren and a heart for the Lord and people. She learned basic computer skills and wanted to help in our work. For four years she took over our newsletter tasks, maintaining the address list and printing labels. After I'd write and format our letter, Sue would take it to the printer and see that it was folded, stuffed and mailed out. It saved us hours. Is there a "Sue" God has called to share this part of your ministry?

WRAP

Recruit a core team to share the work of support raising. With their special gifts they can take key tasks and multiply your effectiveness. As God calls you to ministry, he calls these people too. Chart out what your ministry needs. Go over your segmented prospect list and contact plans for who might want to be part of your core team for the coming year or term of service. When that term is complete, recognize them for the difference they've made. We weren't meant to do it on our own.

14

When Women Raise Support
by Donna Wilson

After two years of doing volunteer work, Rachel decided to quit her job and take a full-time position with a nonprofit that works with inner-city kids. Her new ministry position required her to fundraise, so she began meeting with prospects and enthusiastically sharing her ministry plan. She was invited to speak about her ministry at an adult Sunday-school class at her church, and afterward, John, a young professional, expressed a lot of interest in her ministry. They made plans to meet for lunch to go through Rachel's case statement. As she came to the end of her presentation, Rachel asked John if he would be willing to be one of her ministry partners and would consider giving $50-75 a month to the ministry. John responded that he was eager to partner with her and asked if that meant he would be seeing her on a regular basis. Rachel explained that she would be sending a regular newsletter and hoped to keep in touch by phone or in person as she was able. But John responded that he was thinking of something more like dinner and a movie.

Susan never knew anything about God until she got to college. There she became a Christian through involvement in a campus ministry. Sharing Christ with her friends was soon her passion, and after graduation she felt strongly that God was calling her to continue to work with students on staff with the campus ministry. During college she had attended a church near the campus that had welcomed her when she was new in the faith. Susan met with the chairman of the church's mission committee to ask if the church would support her work so other students like herself could come to the Lord. The committee chair listened quietly as she talked about the needs on campus and her vision for reaching students. Finally he responded that he was very supportive of a ministry on the campus and that the church was anxious to see students come to the Lord, but that the church believed that Scripture taught that women should not hold ministry positions unless it was with children or other women. Therefore the church could not support her work.

SOME THINGS ARE JUST DIFFERENT

Fund development is hard work regardless of your gender, but women face some unique issues. Our training frequently does not prepare us for them, and they are issues that can stop us dead in our tracks if we haven't taken the time to think them through. In addition, there are also fund development issues that are not unique to women, but that seem to be aggravated by the differences between men and women. Our internal responses, our patterns of thinking and our self-concepts are all woven into who God has created us to be as women. Although many of these issues are not specifically about fundraising but rather center around issues of being a woman in ministry, they seem to surface most distinctly (and painfully) in the fundraising process.

The issues are varied, but most of them tend to fall into one of five categories: theological issues, issues of value, issues of self-doubt, issues of being a wife/mother or single, and issues of sexuality.

Theological Issues

After years of debate the positions on the role of women in ministry are diverse. While some portions of Scripture make statements that seem to clearly prohibit women from taking certain ministry roles, other portions tell stories of God using women in those very roles. The apostle Paul, who makes the most specific statements about women, can also be seen trusting important aspects of ministry to them.

Women who are beginning to raise funds to do ministry need to be clear on what Scripture says about women's roles and what they believe God has called them to. It is critical that they come to a personal place of comfort and conviction before they begin to invite others into partnership. If you are unsure of the validity of your ministry, it is nearly impossible to raise funds for it.

1. Work through the issues yourself first. Study the arguments for various positions and understand why they are held. Read those who have done serious scholarship in this area. Be familiar with scriptural models of women who followed God's call. Become confident in what you believe first and convinced of his call in your life.

2. Don't get defensive. Don't try to change a prospect's position or debate it in a fundraising call. Offer to continue the conversation at another time. If this is a long-term relationship, you may want to look for ways you can graciously widen their perspective a bit, but don't expect change to happen quickly.

3. Focus on the impact of the ministry and what you are hoping to accomplish. If you are comfortable, invite a supportive male colleague or supervisor who can affirm your role to visit the donor with you. Let them see God's work through you in the lives of those you are ministering to.

Issues of Value

Another scenario that married women in ministry encounter goes like this:

> *Yes, we are really convinced that what you are doing is wonderful. We're so glad you're out there carrying on this important ministry. But why do you need to raise money? Shouldn't you just volunteer your time? After all, your husband has a job.*

The version for the single woman is slightly different:

Since you don't have a family your expenses are obviously much lower, and you shouldn't need a full salary.

When women confront this thinking, it calls into question the value of their ministry at a very personal level. It creates guilt feelings and makes them worry that they are being greedy or materialistic. It also raises questions for many women about the importance of their ministry as compared to a male coworker and whether it merits compensation. Interestingly, I've never heard of anyone suggesting to a man that he shouldn't be paid because his wife had a job. Yet well-meaning donors often make these statements without thinking of their impact.

At this point we need to return to Scripture and look at ministry from God's perspective. Both Christ himself and the apostle Paul affirmed the principle that those who labor spiritually should be supported materially by the people of God (Lk 10:7; 1 Cor 9:3-11; 1 Tim 5:18). A laborer is worthy of her wages.

Issues of Self-Doubt

The questions women ask themselves may be tougher than those asked by others. As I talk with women in ministry from different parts of the country and of different ages, I find most struggle to overcome the whispered lies of the evil one that we are unworthy and unloved. We have learned to compensate by working hard and hiding our self-doubt with business and accomplishment. But these coping mechanisms break down when we are faced with hard questions asked by our donors or when we find ourselves meeting with the high-powered prospect who makes us feel incompetent. This seems to be especially true as we move into contexts that are decidedly male in style, such as the corporate world or church finance committees.

When this happens, a helpful approach is to apply whatever cross-cultural ministry training we may have. As missionaries we are "bridge" people connecting nonbelievers and Christians, dominant and minority societies and, in this case, people with resources and people with needs. As in our work, we know that cultural differences inevitably cause dissonance in the form of frustration, misunderstanding, confusion, tension and embarrassment. However, our "entry posture" or approach to the situation can be critical to the outcome. Cross-cultural training encourages us to come with openness, acceptance, trust and adaptability. How do these positions apply to building a support team for your ministry?

Openness. As we move into intimidating situations, we need first to open ourselves in prayer. It is critical to take prayer seriously not only in our ministry, but also in resourcing that ministry. Recruit friends who will pray for you, especially as you are in the midst of a presentation or meeting. Second, be open to believe God will be at work and expect him to grow you through this experience, whether or not you receive a positive response. And if a prospect makes you feel intimidated or insecure, don't assume it's because you are a woman. Chances are high that your male coworker would also be intimidated by this person.

Acceptance. Acceptance involves being able to accept both the other person and ourselves. When we accept ourselves as God created us, we operate out of confidence. We know that we are called by God to this ministry, and God's call is the source of our boldness. God has equipped us with gifts to do the task that he has called us to. We are professionals in his work.

We also need to have an attitude of acceptance toward the prospect, despite his or her weaknesses. People who talk over you or who control all situations are usually people who, at the core, are themselves insecure. Their intimidating ways compensate and cover their own fears. Pray for them and accept them as people God loves.

Trust. When we have a case of nerves, we often blurt out our agenda and look for a way to leave the room as quickly as possible. So rather than focus first on what you want, start out by showing a genuine interest in your donor. Most people are hungry to be truly listened to. Ask questions about them, their interests and their passions or pains. This will build trust and equip you to speak to those topics by highlighting how your ministry intersects with their interests or concerns.

Adaptability. Be willing to adapt to the culture of the world you have entered when you make a support-raising call. If it is the business world, learn what you can about business protocol. Dress professionally. This doesn't mean you have to invest lots of money in new clothes, but it does mean you need at least one outfit that looks good and you feel good in. If you're not good with outfits, get help from a friend with good taste who works in a corporate setting. If you're unsure about what's appropriate, ask ahead about the dress code in the office you will be visiting. In today's business world you might encounter anything from suits to khakis to jeans.

Be prepared. Do your homework on the prospect, on your proposal and on your presentation. Practice so you can be clear and concise. Remember that time is worth money, so honor your prospect by staying within the agreed time frame.

After we enter with these postures we need to employ positive crosscultural coping skills of observing, listening and inquiring. As women we should make the most of our natural female strengths (listening, understanding, awareness of other's feelings, collaboration, consensus gaining) to create rapport and empathy not only for our benefit, but also for the prospect.

Issues of Being a Wife/Mother/Single

In few other jobs does your marital status become an issue. In fact, in most states it is illegal to even take one's marital status into consideration when hiring for a position. However, ministry is not a matter of "putting up the numbers." Character and values, not just skills, will be evaluated by some prospective donors. Thus we, as women in ministry, find our personal lives become a central issue in the process of recruiting donors to our cause. We will be asked how will we balance family and ministry life or how we as single women will provide for ourselves.

It is true that Scripture teaches the importance of the role of the body of Christ in living our lives, and most donors asking those questions seem to have well-intentioned concerns. Yet men in ministry are rarely asked the same questions unless it becomes obvious that they are unusually absent in the name of their ministry. Issues of personal, emotional, spiritual and family health are ones both men and women are called to be responsible for.

Ministry is not just a job; it is a calling. It's important we help our donors see our ministry as something we do in obedience to God and not for our own ego. By doing so we affirm and model the importance of obedience to God for our spouse, our children or (if we are single) our family and friends. A healthy Christian home is a powerful source of confidence and credibility.

Marriage, parenting and ministry. As women seeking to follow God, we need to affirm the importance of the family and our roles as wives and mothers. When asked by donors we should be able to talk about the ways we are honoring that commitment in our personal lives. How have we worked out child-care, family time, nurturing, teaching our children about God and spending time growing our relationship with our spouse? How can they pray for us and support us as we work to balance two very important roles God has called us to?

Differentiate between a high view of family and "family idolatry." Share with your donor ways your ministry helps to build your family, for instance, Christian role models for kids, special times at camps or conferences, opportunities to see God at work and answering prayer, God's trustworthiness in providing for the family and exciting examples of faith.

If "family idolatry" is one extreme, "marketplace idolatry" is the other. While some traditional churches prefer mothers to have no paid role in ministry, the trend is for too many Christian mothers (and fathers) to build careers at the expense of their children, hiring nannies in the same way they hire gardeners and housekeepers. The open Christian home where there is mutual support for ministry and the children are truly parented is biblical rejection of both extremes.

Singleness and ministry. While most donors don't worry about family matters for single people, they may question the wisdom of pursuing a career that does not offer high pay or financial security for a woman who is not married. Sometimes they feel "responsible" for you and may be giving out of that motivation rather than God's call. That's a big reason to build a link beyond yourself to the people you're reaching, as we describe in the next chapter.

Donors who see you as a "poor thing" may drop their support if you decide to marry. In these situations it is important to remind both ourselves and our donors that God is our provider and it is in him alone that we have confidence and security. Their financial partnership with us is a way they can participate in what God is doing through our ministry.

Whether single, married or parenting, there are complex issues that women in ministry must balance. Take advantage of the power of your community: meet with other women in ministry and learn from each other. If there aren't natural opportunities in the context of your ministry, look around your church or community for other women in ministry and start your own group that can encourage, pray for and support one another. Or find a woman who can act as a mentor and advisor with whom you can meet on a regular basis. Don't be a "lone ranger" in ministry. Connectedness is important for everyone, but especially for women.

Issues of Sexuality

Although we'd like to believe that this isn't a problem among Christians, history and the daily news remind us that we are all fallen creatures and subject to temptation. In random surveys of women in ministry, I found more than twenty-five percent had encountered a fundraising situation that involved some kind of difficult experience with sexual overtones. These have ranged from simple feelings of discomfort to more overt inappropriate behavior. More than one single woman has told me of male prospects who have agreed to an appointment, or even financial support, in hopes of getting a date.

When Christ sent out his followers to do ministry, he told them to be "wise as serpents and innocent as doves" (Mt 10:16 NRSV). We want to function neither with suspicion or naiveté, but rather to use good planning and practice to avoid a difficult situation.

First, minimize the possibility of misinterpretation by being clear and direct. Be professional and focus on the ministry. Be clear that this is about the mission, not about you. Avoid meeting with a male prospect alone. If he is married, try to schedule a meeting with him and his wife. She may be interested in your work in her own right. If he is single or divorced, bring along a mutual friend, a coworker or young person you work with. Meet in a public place and be sure the agenda is clear ahead of time.

Be positive. Expect the best. If something is said you are uncomfortable with, remember that the ball is in your court regarding how you will respond. Familiarize yourself with information that is written about communication styles of men and women. This can help you be more confident in interpreting signals accurately. Enlist the help of a male supervisor, coworker or friend. Practice your presentation with them and get their feedback.

Finally, don't overlook the wonderful potential among women donors. Consider putting together a prospect list to form a team of women who will not only pray for you and give to your ministry, but who also will become active in recruiting other women to become involved. These women can become not only bridge builders but also fundraisers on your behalf.

GO OUT IN CONFIDENCE

It is a great privilege and joy to be a woman called by God to minister to his people. It is even more of a privilege to carry out that role in the context of a team of people who pray for you, encourage you and support your work financially. Because God is the one who has called us, loved us and equipped us, we can confidently invite others to join in the process and be a part of what he is doing through us.

Part Four
Developing Your Team

You actually asked for money. Now what? Here's how to move with your donors toward the future God has for your ministry.

Build Partnership

Send Mail

Ask Again

Get Sent for Good

15

Build
Partnership

He said *"Yes, we'll support your work." What should I do now?*
She said, "No, we like your work but can't help you now."
What should I do now?
We showed them our case statement last time. We don't have
anything new to show them. What should we do now?

You've made a home in a supportive church. You've sent the letters,
made the phone calls and met with your prospects. You've asked for
money and survived. Along the way you've found a core support team
who will share some of the tasks with you.

It's likely that over half of your funding comes from fifteen to twenty
people. What can you do to increase their joy in partnering with your
ministry? Do they want more than an annual thank-you note and a
prayer letter? Yes they do, and working with them is the heart of what
you'll do from here forward. But how do you know what they expect?
How can you connect meaningfully year after year? And how much time
does it take? Since time is every missionary's highest felt need, let's take
that question first.

TIME AND MONEY: THE FOCUS PHILOSOPHY

"Doctor, do I have to floss all my teeth?" asks a child. "No, only the ones you want to keep." Experts tell missionaries to pay attention to all their donors. But you can't do your job and pay the same amount of time to them all. In chapter seven you learned that they don't want you to. What do you do?

☐ Send your newsletter to everyone on your list.

☐ People who give less than $500 a year and don't volunteer in any capacity should also receive a personal note of thanks each year, an occasional phone call and invitations to promotional events.

☐ Those with potential to give $50 to $200 a month or greater should get, in addition to the notes and periodic phone calls, a face-to-face visit with you once or twice a year if you're working in North America.

☐ People with potential to give $3,000 a year or more and who live within a couple of hours of your ministry should see you four times a year. One of those visits is to ask for funds; three are to pursue the relationship as your donor wants to define it. Bear in mind that if the donor is Asian-American, you are not asking face to face but through letter or an older intermediary. If you're overseas, this means inviting your top donors to travel to your ministry and a rich array of communication during the year.

Don't floss all your teeth. It's impossible to pay the same level of attention to everybody. Go deeper with the smaller group rather than trying to sustain hundreds of relationships. Accept the fact that you'll lose some donors; ten percent a year is normal. If your home base is one city and you move to another to do youth work or urban outreach, your financial future is going to be in the city of your ministry. Focusing on your top twenty is the best way to replace those losses and grow your funding. You can do that, and the rest of your support work, in thirty to forty days a year.

"I fundraise five percent of the time, but I think about it fifty percent of the time," said a veteran missionary. For over three hundred days a year you shouldn't think about fundraising. Go to your supervisor and ask for help to find the slower times in the ministry year that are best for building donor relationships.

GETTING TO KNOW YOU, GETTING TO KNOW ALL ABOUT YOU

We've mentioned the focus philosophy of concentrating on a "top fifteen" or twenty. Now let's focus in even closer: think through your relationships with the top five people (including churches, foundations or other major sources) who could give the most to support your ministry. They may not yet be donors or may give modestly now, but you think there might be interest. Open your contact plans (chapter eight) for each individual. What do you know about him or her? Go over each point below. Then expand on your contact plan form. Enter the information on the contact plan or in a separate word processing file.

We're looking for links between the person and your ministry. When you discover those links you can strengthen them. You'll find creative ways of building the relationship not merely with yourself but with your vision.

Personal
☐ background
☐ Christian conversion/spiritual milestones
☐ church
☐ church roles
☐ Christian activity outside church
☐ family: marriage, children (ages)
☐ spouse's interests
☐ education
☐ children's education
☐ children's Christian experience
☐ recreation
☐ vacations
☐ reading
☐ hobbies
☐ health concerns

Professional

□ vocation
□ company
□ job title
□ how long in the company
□ professional accomplishments
□ professional association memberships, roles

Charitable/Ministry Interests

□ social and political concerns
□ community service (organizations, roles, titles)
□ friends of yours who know him/her
□ contact with your kind of ministry
□ contact with your agency (who, where, when, what)
□ first gift to your agency
□ last gift, if any, to your agency
□ when and how he/she prefers to give
□ any noncash gifts
□ what values does he/she hold that your ministry affirms
□ if asked, how he/she answered: What do you expect from the ministries you support?

FROM ME TO THE MINISTRY

For many of your donors, their concern for your ministry begins with you and stops there. While that's a good beginning, a deep partnership will evolve as you lead your donors beyond yourself to a direct relationship with the work. Not all of your donors want that, but all of them should receive the invitation.

Let's say you're in a high-school ministry and have a friendship with a supporter. Beyond telling him or her how you and the work are doing, seek a personal meeting where you can do one or more of the following:
□ Ask for evaluation of ideas, plans or reports according to your donor's skill level and interest.

☐ Give reports on your work that relate especially to his or her area of concern.

☐ Ask for an increased gift or extra gift for a project.

☐ Ask for labor or fundraising help.

☐ Recognize what the donor's done and what he or she means to your ministry.

☐ Conduct an on-site visit to your school to check out the scene and meet students, teachers or administrators.

☐ Invite the donor to be a guest at a camp or weekend event sponsored by your agency.

Once you've given your donor a glimpse of the scene and learned more about his or her skills and interests, extend the invitation to take part directly by

☐ mentoring, tutoring, or discipling a high-school student

☐ volunteering with teen moms

☐ sharing at a club meeting

☐ meeting with seniors to talk about transition to college or work

As involvement grows, let your donor know needs beyond the annual gift. High-school works need people who can

☐ meet with some other partners to pray for the school

☐ give scholarships for camps and special programs

☐ loan homes or vehicles for a retreat

☐ labor: hospitality, office work, rides to meetings or conferences

☐ fundraise: committee work, introductions, events

All along the way, the bond can also be nurtured by your high schoolers. Simple ways to make an impact include

☐ a thank-you note for a scholarship to camp

☐ a student-sponsored party for parents and donors at end of the year

☐ a letter telling him or her what the ministry has meant in the student's life. A graduate wrote:

> *I was in Bible club for many years, and that helped with school, with setting goals for the future and with all of life. Bible club gave me a chance to learn about God but didn't push me. . . . It opened a new world for me and gave me a chance to see different things.*

Fundraising professionals call this cultivation, but it's nothing more than developing a relationship, discovering your gifts and responding together to God's call.

What if you don't have geography going for you? Consider the case of a church-planting mission to an unreached people in Asia. First there are the basics:

☐ getting a phone connection

☐ e-mailing reports and a letter sent by your volunteer at home

☐ inviting your donor to dust off the old passport and visit

☐ sending a letter (translated) from someone in a local church

☐ asking your agency to send him or her a letter of appreciation for helping

You actually stimulate vision and excitement by asking for more than that annual or monthly gift (more on this in chapter seventeen). Let your needs be known. It may be

☐ an increased gift or extra gift for a project

☐ help arranging visits home: lining up medical or dental appointments, desserts or church meetings

☐ "adopting" a church, family or a new convert for intercession

☐ needed in-kind gifts: Bibles, medical supplies, clothing, computer support as feasible and appropriate to your mission

COME AND SEE

Nothing beats seeing the work, walking where you walk, to move the donor relationship from you only to you and the ministry. I recently had the fun of introducing a businessman to a local outreach to kids. He saw the messy desks and second-hand equipment in the headquarters. He met the young graduate of an elite school who'd joined the staff to work for Peace Corps pay. He met the blue jeans-attired director and saw the glow in the faces of kids from different races in a Bible club. Two hours changed his life. Though he said nothing to me at the time, a little later he not only gave a four-figure gift but recruited a friend to come, see and give as well.

Your top prospects, your pastor and your missions contact person should all be asked to "come and see." Local missionaries don't need to put on special programs. Overseas missionaries don't need to host two-week work projects. Just invite good people to walk in your steps for a short time. The site can be across town or across an ocean. People who see are never the same.

What's right for your donors? Pray and brainstorm with two or three other workers in your organization. Then write your plans into the "Next Steps" section of the contact plan for each of your top twenty.

Asking is just the end of the beginning. Now the fun begins. Have a dream for your donors to achieve a partnership that goes past you to those you are serving in Christ's name. Seek their joy in connecting with your work. You'll learn what Paul meant, "Not that I seek the gift, but I seek the profit that accumulates to your account" (Phil 4:17 NRSV).

WRAP

"Fundraising is a relational process guided by a vision." Keep that process going. Set aside thirty to forty days a year for your support team. What do you know about your prospects? What have they seen of the ministry? How can you put handles on your work that go beyond financial giving? As you seek answers to these questions, you'll get the insights you need to nourish the "donor bond." The first gift is just the end of the beginning.

In the same way, when you're inviting new prospects to consider your work, don't rush for a gift. Keep your focus on building the relationship: *you see people who will be friends of your ministry for a long time.* Listen, share what matters to you and figure out what he or she wants to do. Some may question the time it takes and say, "Ask now. You're leaving money on the table." But as one Latino Young Life director replied, "I don't care if I leave money on the table because I'm never leaving the table."

16

Send Mail

It's January 19, and I still haven't sent out half our Christmas letters. It seems impersonal unless I write a note on each one. My donors must think I'm ungrateful, but how can anyone do the job and keep up with this?

Every six weeks your donors should hear from you. The hard news is that if you do less than that, you'll lose support. But how can you maintain that level of contact without diverting too much time from your ministry?

In chapter fifteen on partnership you have a strategy for connecting personally with your donors. Here we'll describe how to nourish that with a mix of letters, notes and e-communication that lets you maintain your ministry and sanity. Last we'll advise on how to write a letter when you're in a financial jam. Set aside eight, two-day blocks of time for correspondence in your annual calendar. Plan to mail your Christmas letter by December 5 so it's not washed away in the year-end postal tidal wave. Send your last letter thirty days before the fiscal-year close.

WRITING FOR READERS

While some missionaries are naturals with the written word, most of us have to labor to construct a clear sentence. Here are tips for the majority.

Write to a person, not a crowd. Ask the Lord to help you picture one or two of the people with whom you most want to communicate. With your reader in mind, look at the previous letter you wrote and the last letter your agency sent out. Did you share a need? Then you'll want to bring your reader up-to-date. Did you emphasize a particular part of your work? Maybe you should let him know about another. What's the last personal communication you had?

Don't split the agenda. Don't mention money unless that's your main topic. Prayer letters are for prayer. Too many letters end with a word about how deep in the red the missionary is.

Devote a letter to that topic and send it after you've asked your Number One and Number Two prospects by voice—phone or face to face. The wrong timing can cost you money.

With money out of the way, think of the ministry. Who is changing as a result? What touches you most deeply? Try to put in a sentence what you'd like your reader most to know about the work right now.

Pick a story that illustrates your point. It can be a story of success or failure, but it should illustrate your mission. Begin your letter with that story. You can include an occasional meditation in your letter, but sermons are usually a bore to your readers. A "teaching" letter means you've forgotten your individual reader.

Be specific. Compare these two stories from China. Version one is general:

We toured a monastery. The guide said that Jesus was not real but that Buddha was. These people really need the gospel. God opened the door for me to share with our translator, who was probably a communist. That evening at dinner, I asked him about spiritual things. Carol gave her testimony, and he asked for a Bible the next day. Yet sometimes the Chinese officials talk with you about Christianity just to be polite. God can still work in these situations.

As I read that, I have no sense of the monastery, the translator or personal intensity in the missionary or his guide.

Version two is specific:

The smell of incense and old yak butter made the dimly lit shrines seem oppressive. I was piqued at our guide's closing remark, "The world has three major religions, and Islam and Christianity are not true because only Buddha was a real person." Mr. S., our translator, whispered, "You might want to dispute that, but not here."

That evening over supper I asked him, "What were your feelings as you walked through the monastery?" He was diplomatic. "I'm not religious, but we Chinese respect the culture of our minority people." He didn't reply, so I came in harder. "But what if these customs are based on superstition? As a Christian, I could not have good feelings for a religious system not based on truth and that causes people to worship a man like you or me."

At that point he said, "Can you tell me about Christianity? I don't know very much." Carol shared, too, of how Jesus gave her courage and hope through the times of the death of her father and Steve. Tears came to Mr. S's eyes. We talked until the restaurant was empty and the owner anxious to lock up. The next day, he asked if he could correspond with us and if we could give him a Chinese-English Bible. While he's a member of the Party who may have wanted to be polite, we trust God is at work in him.

Specifics convey the power in a letter.

Once your story is vivid, less is more. Have mercy on your reader; remember where she is when she opens the mail. If your letter is longer than one and a half pages, she will read it later or never.

Show your reader where to find your main point. Use nice wide margins, spaces between paragraphs, boxes, shadows and bullet points to set off key messages. Or if you don't like all that boxy stuff, use a nice large font and lots of white space for an easy read.

Don't get hung up on personalizing each letter. It's more important to get them sent. One missionary says,

We used to send four long letters a year with personal messages. Each letter was a three-day project. People would say, "We haven't heard from

you in a long time." We switched to short letters six to eight times, no
personal notes. Now they say, "You sure do keep in touch."

Of course people like your notes. A little comment, "Hope that new
job is going well" or "Thanks for that e-mail message; it was a real
encouragement," ups the chance your letter will be read. Hold back
nine or ten letters from each mailing to pen some personal comment.
Don't just write "Thanks for your prayers" on letter after letter. That's
not personal, just time-consuming. Err on the side of getting the
news out.

☐ Use e-mail for urgent news or prayer requests. Resist the urge to
circulate humor and columns of political polemics. Some of your donors
get one hundred e-mails a day at work.

☐ Each year send each donor a quality, personally written thank-you
letter or card.

☐ Write your draft, let it sit overnight and edit it; then let a friend
proofread it. You'll be stunned by the improvements.

FREQUENTLY ASKED QUESTIONS

Should I send a business reply envelope in every letter?
Yes, for "felt need" ministries like helping inner-city kids. You want to make
it as easy as possible for someone to give if they are moved. But for college
ministries that are more strategic, it just deadens the impact. Send an
envelope in December and June or the last month of your fiscal year or when
there's a real crisis.

What about photos and scanners?
An image of some kind, while not needed each time, is a big help when you're
not a natural writer. Three or four photos across the year to illustrate the
work are great. Your beautiful portrait once a year will do just *fine*. Make the
photo sufficiently close up to show the eyes of your subject, not the common
group silhouette.
Scanned photos are OK provided you have enough contrast. Pay your local
printer a few dollars for the highest-quality scan or ask to see the alternatives.
So far, nothing beats a half-tone black and white photo for resolution. Allow
your print shop a few days to get it done.

What's a good software program?
Technology will obsolete us by the time this book goes to print, but our

choices today would be Microsoft Publisher or ClarisWorks for ease of use. If it costs more than $100 or takes more than a day to learn the program, don't get it.

How much identification goes on my personal prayer letter?

I've got a great letter here from Melanie. I think she does inner-city work, but I don't know where, with what organization or even her last name. I tossed away her envelope out of habit, so I can't send a gift even if I wanted to. Use a header to identify the date of your letter and your agency, a footer to include your name, address, phone and e-mail.

How large should I let my list get?

How many people can you keep in touch with? You'll hear experts that say, "the bigger the better," but most personal letter lists we've seen get less productive after they top three hundred. Decide based on a focus philosophy: twenty to thirty percent of your donors will give seventy to eighty percent of your funds. Some send a Christmas letter to hundreds but others send their regular letter to no more than 150.

Add people who show interest in your work. Reading your letters prepares them for a future invitation to give. After a few years of nonresponse, don't throw away the name but put it in the "inactive" file.

Why don't most people return my stamped and self-addressed cards?

"If you want to receive my mailings, please return the enclosed card with the box checked." The youth worker who sent this has sixty donors and a mailing list of two hundred. Twenty-two people returned her card. The rest said by their actions that they did not feel her form-letter request really required an answer or did not want to add another office task to their day.

First class costs a lot. What about using bulk mail?

If you can, use your agency's nonprofit first-class mail status. If you're on your own, first class is worth the cost. Bulk mail arrives slowly and doesn't forward or return mail when your reader moves. With an average of ten percent of us moving each year, you're losing a lot of people. In fact, the Direct Marketing Association says that over eleven percent of all bulk mail *is never even delivered.* First class is worth it, and your reader doesn't need to boot up the computer to read it.

I'm stuck. Help!

First, go to your agency. Ask the office for half a dozen of the best letters they have on file. Every group has someone who's really gifted at telling stories that go right to the heart of the mission and the reader. Who has that reputation in your organization?

Second, look at letters you get from other ministries and set aside a few you like. What do you like about them? You learned to ride a bike by using training wheels. Then you learned to balance. You fell once or twice, but you got the hang of it. Eventually your letters have to be in your own voice. So train up and then launch out. Don't let the central office write through you.

Third, try to make the setting as pleasant as possible. When do you think most creatively? Morning? Late at night? Does a little John Coltrane or Mozart in the background make it easier to compete with the sirens and lawn blowers? Does a fresh pot of coffee help?

Next, get out a large yellow pad. Think over what has moved you in recent days and weeks. Look at your prayer journal and your last prayer letter. What comes to your heart and mind? Write down names, places, events, notions. Do you see a common thread? Just start writing and see what comes up. Create a rotten first draft; then come back after a soda for another look. Anne Lamott knows the feeling and the only way out.

> *Thirty years ago my older brother, who was ten years old at the time, was trying to get a report on birds written that he'd had three months to write, which was due the next day. We were out at our family cabin in Bolinas, and he was at the kitchen table close to tears, surrounded by binder paper and pencils and unopened books on birds, immobilized by the hugeness of the task ahead. Then my father sat down beside him, put his arm around my brother's shoulder and said, "Bird by bird, buddy. Just take it bird by bird."*[1]

With your yellow pad on the table, your Father sits beside you.

What About the Web?
At this writing, web use is evolving quickly. Large numbers of people over the age of fifty now use the web for shopping and financial planning. Your agency should have a competent, easy-to-navigate site that features your own work on it somewhere.

With the right skills you can build a good web page, but be sure you get your agency's sign-off on it first. E-speech is public speech, and you need to follow the rules of etiquette and your organization's guidelines for public relations.

Web use is better for "pull" than "push." If you need to get information from your agency, the Web lets you find it. If someone needs the services of your ministry to the point that they go looking, a good web site is a marvel. For instance, Christian parents of high-school seniors check web sites of college Christian groups. But if you're trying to awaken interest in the first place, you have to get in front of people personally.

MAYDAY, MAYDAY, WE'VE BEEN HIT

When you take a relational approach to fundraising and ask for commitments before your next fiscal year, you'll rarely have to write a crisis letter, and people will listen when you do. Be as honest and clear as you can. Avoid a split agenda; don't tuck this in with a "regular" prayer letter. Here's what Noel Becchetti, President of Center for Student Missions, sent to his readers when he was in a jam.

You're going to hate this letter. I mean, let's face it. If you're like me, you open letters from donor-supported ministries with that little trickle of fear: "Am I going to be hit with—The Appeal?" That's why I know you're going to hate this letter. I've got to talk to you about Faith Promise, Your Pledge of Support, Standing Behind Our Ministry—*in other words, money.*

First, let me set the context. In 1996, the Center for Student Missions had a good year. Actually, we had a very good year. For which we're grateful. And ministry-wise, 1997 is looking great. . . . Furthermore, our serving groups pay to work with us. About sixty-five percent of our total revenues come from our groups. So we're even more grateful to see how God continues to grow our ministry.

But the remaining thirty-five percent of our funds come through donations. And for some reason, financial support for Kyle and me has dropped off significantly this year.

Fortunately, being a mature guy, I've taken this well ("Everyone hates us! I'm incompetent! We're doomed!"). And we're not alone. Giving has dropped for nearly all of our staff, enabling me to make a thoughtful, reasoned assessment of the overall situation ("We're all doomed! AAAAHHHH!!!").

Hysterics aside, there are four things [SEND MONEY!] I'd like to run by you [SEND MONEY!] related to our current [SEND MONEY!] situation that hopefully will be beneficial [SEND!] and [MONEY!] instructive to both of us:

1. Bottom line, God supplies our needs. Dealing with finances reminds me that all aspects of our work depend on the Lord. It's humbling, and to be honest, the humble thing doesn't come easy for me. But God is reinforcing this lesson in my life.

2. Times like these cause me to especially appreciate the ongoing commitment of our faithful prayer and financial supporters. THANK YOU!

3. If you've been a supporter of CSM in the past, or it's something you have thought about, we could use your help. Thanks for considering it.

4. I promise that I'll bring up requests like this one only when we really need to make them.

That's the story from here. We are truly grateful to God for how he's blessed CSM... and how we've been blessed with you, our partners.

So while, if you're like me, you hated getting this letter, I appreciate your taking the time to read it. I promise to share more cool stories about ministry in the city in future letters—and less about You Know What. Take care and God bless.

The Lord blessed this letter, and CSM's friends rose up and funded the whole need.

WRAP

Enter dates in your calendar for producing your prayer letter. Give your letter assistants plenty of advance notice.

Ask the Lord to guide you and look to him when you get stuck. Write your letter to one or two donors. Begin with a story. Give enough detail in the story to pull your reader in; then be ruthless with yourself and keep it short. Make money the subject only once a year unless your work is in crisis.

Write your letter in four stages. Do a draft, look at it the next day, ask a friend to proofread it, and then do a final edit.

Use special stationery or a card to thank each donor annually. Restrict e-mail to prayer requests or urgent news. When you're in a financial crisis, lay the facts out and ask for help. Your readers will bless you.

17

Ask Again

Ask Sharon for more? That sounds like I'm not thankful for what she's doing already.

People should know our costs go up just like theirs. Why don't they automatically increase their gift?

Jeff stopped giving two months ago. I wonder what I did wrong.

These statements were made by missionaries. In contrast, look at these comments by donors.

We were so moved to hear about the new vision. We can't do all we'd like to do, but we'll increase.

We're making more money this year, so our giving will rise. Where shall we put it?

I lost that return envelope. But I haven't heard from Jon, so maybe he doesn't need my help anymore.

If ever donors and missionaries held different views, it's on the issue of asking for increased support from the current giver. But a partnership can't advance unless you ask people to give again, and *the two most responsive sources of more funding are current and former donors, not new prospects.*

Why don't we ask for more from our donors? We let old fears kick in and forget why they gave in the first place. In this chapter we'll show why and how to ask our current support team members to increase their giving and how to invite our former donors to rejoin the team.

WHY WOULD THEY WANT TO?

In 1990 the bottom fell out of the real estate market and with it went almost thirty percent of our funding. I'd made few requests for increases and had to learn fast. We asked thirty of our supporters to increase, and twenty-nine did. We don't do that each year, but it made us look at the issue. Here's a more typical first-gift-to-next-gift flow.

After a first gift thank your donor and ask about the kind of relationship he'd like to have with your mission. Follow through on that, keeping in touch until a few months before the new fiscal year starts. Then it's time to call again. Old fears may return. When they do, consider these questions.

Why did your donor come on board in the first place? Because you stand for values he believes in, because he trusts you, because through you your donor makes a difference in human lives and glorifies the Lord. He would probably like to make a bigger impact with his giving. Asking for an increase shows him how.

Without challenge, relationships grow stale. If your work is growing and your needs are too, invite your supporter to come with you. Since your donor receives joy from knowing you're making a difference to people, we can see why most new money comes from the same people. It's exciting to be part of something that's going somewhere. If you're not asking for more, you may be subtly saying that your work is static. As you look at the individuals who fund your work, ask yourself why they give and then you'll know how to ask thoughtfully.

Kim Klein puts it well:

We call a donor who has given three or four times over the course of one or two years a "habitual" donor. This person sees himself or herself as part of the organization, even though probably not a big part. Next, the habitual donor is asked personally for a larger gift; if he or she responds with a larger gift than he or she has given before, this person becomes a "thoughtful" donor.[1]

Asking for larger and different gifts makes the donor think about why she gave in the first place and builds commitment to your cause. Givers want you to come back and ask again.

HOW TO ASK FOR AN INCREASE

1. Review your donor reports for the last eight months or more.

2. Make a note by the names of donors who are in financial crisis. Don't ask these people for increased support right now.

3. Open your priority prospect list and update it. What gift level would be right for each person for the coming year? How close would that bring you to your goal?

4. Phone your priority Number One and Number Two people for an appointment to update them on the vision and the budget for the coming year. They might not yet giving at a Number Two level but they have the potential for it as best you can tell.

5. Mail a letter to your priority Number Three people.

Whether you are sharing your case statement for the new year or writing a letter, thank your donors for what their gift helped to accomplish in the last year. Then state in a simple sentence your main ministry goal for the coming year, which shows why you need funds.

We have an invitation to start ministry in two sororities, but I can't go yet because I'm part-time. Full funding of my budget by September 1 means I can be ready when the students return to campus.

Replacing our vehicle will allow us to reach the other villages reliably, and we'll be able to literally get out from under this jalopy.

Since arrival we've been hit with unexpected costs. Our new budget will take pressure off our family so that we can focus on the people we were sent to reach.

6. Ask for a range of increase, not a single dollar amount. For instance, "Could you consider an increase in the range of $10-30 a month?" If it's an annual gift of $1,000, "Could you consider an increase in the range of $1,200-1,500 this year?"

WHEN TO ASK

For a monthly or quarterly donor, ten months of consistent action is a good interval. For an annual donor, try two or three months before the month of their last gift. If it's a December gift, approach the donor for an increase in October.

You may have folks who increase their gift level without being asked. That's great, but they too need a visit from you to show your appreciation and how your ministry is developing. Even when donors say no to an increase request, you'll find that they say, "We wish we could do more but can't," and often share about their situation. Over time your donors will understand your work much more clearly, and when they're able to help you more, they will.

Most donors' incomes rise annually. If they tithe, they're going to give extra help to those who let them know there's a need. If you go silent on your donors, they won't appreciate you more.

Let people know why you need their help and why you need it now, but remember they give on their own schedule. Observe their style and their timing and try to dovetail it with your fiscal year.

"ONE-TIME" GIFTS

I have lots of one-time gifts but too few monthly gifts. How can I get my donors to give each month?

My friend sent in a check for $500 without a monthly intent-to-give card. Besides writing a thank-you note, how do I respond?

One-time gifts are usually one-time-a-year gifts. In your record-keeping, translate one-time gifts into monthly segments and ask again next year, for example:

Thank you for your support for our ministry last year. It was such a help to getting us started. This year our budget is up eighteen percent to extend our volunteer training program to twenty more kids. Could you help us again this year, with an increase for our new budget?

If you've been keeping your donor up-to-date, you'll probably receive another, higher gift.

DONORS NO MORE?

"Lapsed donor" is the term for someone who has given in the past but stopped. If your friend has a pattern of monthly gifts and then misses a month, he's not "lapsed." Anyone can miss a month. If, however, two months go by with no record of a gift, call him. Without a doubt, calling in these circumstances feels awkward. The good news is that you never have to ask, "Why did you stop giving to our work?"

You don't ever have to say that because most of the time your donor didn't stop giving. I make four or five calls a year to friends who, judging by my donor tracking report, fell off the edge of the earth.

"Ralph, I don't have any record of a gift in the last three months and wondered if everything was OK with you all" (a little awkward but not bad).

Ralph: "Really? We just got back from vacation, and we tried to get our checks mailed out before we left. Hmm, here it is under this pile."

I want to think that Ralph was on the level, but it's not my business to probe. He is kind of disorganized after all. But in a few days we had a check for three months' support.

When your monthly donor is two months late, try this approach:

Hi, this is Sally Jones of CityTeam. Your partnership matters to us, but we couldn't find a record of your February gift. Is it possible that we failed to provide a reply envelope for you?

Once you broach the topic, your friend will explain. Usually it will be due to a financial problem. Sometimes it will be due to relocation and replacing your ministry with one more local.

What about the annual donor whose gift is more than thirty days later than last year? Pick up the phone without delay and say,

> *Your gift last year was a great help to us. We hope you'll be part of our support team again this year. Will that be possible?*

Then listen closely as your friend defines the way she'd like to connect with your work this time around. When a gift is late, it often is late by our standards, not the donor's. Maybe her business has not closed a major deal just yet; maybe she has reorganized her giving calendar. But it's up to the us to ask the question.

When the Check Is Not in the Mail

> *Mr. Thompson said he would give last November. I called him in December, and he said he'd send it by year-end. I called in January and he put me off again. Something's wrong.*

You're right; something *is* wrong. If you were clear in your case presentation and on your agreement and your friend has not given, it's likely that he won't be your donor.

There's no point blaming Mr. Thompson. He probably wanted to give but ran into financial trouble that he prefers not to talk about. Don't take it personally. Be professional, leave Mr. Thompson in the Lord's hands, and take his name off your priority prospect list. Keep sending your letter with a reply envelope.

When the Monthly Gift Isn't Monthly

Many "monthly" gifts aren't. Christian agencies are trying to remedy that with electronic transfer arrangements. This authorizes your organization to deduct an agreed gift amount from your donor's account each month. Offer this service to your donor.

Your organization can help by giving your donors a monthly receipt and reply envelope, including a statement of the total gifts to date or a chart of boxes labeled by the month, with the *gift* months checked off. This shows the donor immediately where he stands in relation to his gift intent.

A growing number of donors, however, prefer to solve the problem themselves through Quicken or other popular software budgeting programs. It leaves the donor in more control of his or her cash flow, sometimes skipping a month intentionally and doubling a gift later. As we've said, there's no cause for concern until you go two months without the check.

But even in this electronic age many groups leave the issue to you, the missionary. Consider one of three approaches. First, send a letter to your regular donors. Describe your situation. Take a look at two examples:

> *Once a year I send out a summary of what you have planned (not "pledged") and what your actual giving has been. It would be very helpful if you were able to fill in any of the "gaps" in your giving as I have planned to budget according to your fulfilling this plan. If circumstances prevent this, know that I will understand. Thanks once again for your financial partnership with me. I thank the Lord for you and pray that this is to your benefit and your blessing.*

Jan	Feb	Mar	Apr	May	Jun	July	Aug	Sep	Oct	Nov	Dec

Figure 17.1. Annual giving checklist

For each individual donor this missionary fills out a chart like that in figure 17.1, with the amounts of gifts and the months they were received and encloses a reply envelope to use in making up missing gifts. Another encloses a separate slip of bright paper, including the chart in figure 17.2, reading

> *Your giving plan for July 2002-June 2003 is _____. Here's my record of your giving through February:*

July	Aug	Sep	Oct	Nov	Dec	Jan	Feb

If your records differ from mine, please contact me so I can investigate any discrepancies. If you've misplaced or don't have a gift remittance envelope, feel free to use the postage-paid business reply envelope enclosed. Thanks so much for your partnership!

Figure 17.2. Six-month giving checklist

A second way to deliver the message is e-mail. The advantage of e-mail is its immediacy. The downside it that it's less tangible and doesn't put the envelope in the hand of your donor.

We favor sending a letter and following up with a phone call. You need that voice contact anyway. Follow the principle of business before pleasure, so bring up the "missing gifts" issue first and ask, "Did you receive our letter about meeting the budget?" It will only take a minute or so and then you can enjoy catching up with your friend.

In Asian-American cultures such a phone call may be unacceptable. If you do phone, just visit and do *not* mention money. Simply express appreciation for help given in the past. Don't worry; your letter will be taken seriously. It will be even stronger if one of your older, respected advocates sends it out on your behalf.

Unhappy Ex-donors

Once in a while a donor will stop giving due to a loss of confidence in your work. She won't often tell you; you'll just notice that her gifts stop. Too many missionaries don't take the initiative to ask her why. While it's no fun to hear, it's always instructive. Think of the discomfort as tuition you've paid and learn all you can. As nondefensively as possible, ask some questions.

□ *I'm not here to change your thinking but to understand why we're not enjoying your support these days. What are you free to share with me about that?*

□ *Are you giving to a similar ministry instead of ours?*

□ *Could I ask why you prefer that organization at this time?*

□ *Can you help me understand where you feel we're on the wrong track?*

□ *What could we do to restore your confidence in our work?*

Your former donor has a story to tell. Listen carefully. If your custom was to meet personally with her, seek a face-to-face meeting. It's a kind of "exit interview." She may prefer not to meet, and she's under no obligation to do so, but her story can really help you improve your work. If you're getting more than one or two such unhappy departees a year, you or your agency has a problem.

Above all, write your departing donor a genuine letter of thanks. Total the amount she's given, and share some way she's blessed you or the people your work touches. Let her go in peace.

Losing a Large Gift

First Baptist gave Tim, a missionary to Belgium, $7,000 a year for three years. During year three they sent Tim a letter saying, "We believe the Lord has called us to give only to missionaries doing church planting in the 10-40 Window. As result we want to let you know that we will redirect your support to a missionary in that area."

Tim could sympathize, aware as he was of the need for missionaries in the 10-40 Window. But it hit him and his wife like a thunderbolt. Already living very simply, replacing their gift wouldn't be easy. After recovering and thinking over the situation, Tim e-mailed back,

> *I know you as people who seek the Lord's will, and I believe he is leading you.*
>
> *I need to share, though, that the sudden loss of a gift as large as yours will have a major negative impact on the work and on me. I will have to leave the family for a month or more to fundraise in the States. This will be a hardship to them, and the trip itself will be costly. Could we ask you for three things? First, could you consider "stepping down" your gift to $2,000 a year instead of dropping your support entirely? Second, pray for us to find new donors and approach the rest of our support team about the new need to increase.*
>
> *Third, pray for the outreach effort to local Muslims currently underway, especially for Ali, who came to our Bible study last night.*
>
> *We need to complete this effort before we can fundraise again. And thanks for all you have done for us. We hope to hear from you soon.*
>
> *In Christ, Tim and Mary*

The church agreed to make the change gradually but never did remove him from their budget. He kept the relationships and still receives a substantial gift each year.

The Lost Are Sometimes Found

I sat with Jack in a coffee shop. He'd helped us for six years, and now his company had filed for bankruptcy. I listened to an ugly story. Expecting me to ask him for a gift again, he said, "There's nothing we can do for you this year."

I responded, "Jack, God's given you wonderful gifts. You'll be back. You're still a partner. Let's keep meeting. When you're able to help again, we'll celebrate."

That morning we celebrated our friendship with prayer and scrambled eggs. Two years later we celebrated with a check.

WRAP

To treat your donors as real partners, you have to ask them to give each year. You don't need to go back to go, asking "Will you give this year?" but you must share your goals and the new budget they require.

Your support team members, current and former, who have written out your agency's name on a check and enclosed a note with your name on it, are far more likely to help you than new prospects. They have a track record of caring about you and your ministry. Share with them your heart, your dreams and your needs. Call them to go with you into the future.

But their giving won't be mechanical. Gifts can be increased, one-time, lapsing, irregular, ungiven, lost or recovered. *Trust in the Lord and open communication with each donor* is the only formula for handling it.

When donors mysteriously vanish, act based on what you do know, not what you don't know. You do know they've helped in the past; you don't know *why* they've stopped. Pray, assume the best and reach out to them. Like the Young Life director quoted in chapter fifteen, never leave the table.

18

Get Sent
for Good

As you build your support team, you'll discover strengths and weakness in yourself and your organization. You'll see success and failure. It's always tempting to look to the organization or your fellow staff or missionaries for the answers ("they woulda-shoulda-coulda"), and our gripes can be right, but ultimately we stand before the Lord. If we want to work for a fast company, maybe a nonprofit is the wrong place to be.

No baseball team, they say, is ever as bad as it looks on a day when it loses. And no team is as good as it looks on the given day when it wins. So it is in developing a team to resource your ministry. You're not a genius because you get one big yes to a request, nor are you a loser because you get a major turn-down. Welcome a no as a tutorial.

WHEN IT GETS HARD

The "big lie" in the Christian world today is that success is from God and that failure is from the devil. In fact, it can be the other way around.

Failure and rejection, Luther said, are "God's alien work" to crucify our self-will so that he can do his "proper work" of raising us up to new life.[1] Unless you and I can welcome the cross, we will be disappointed in God, our organizations, our donors and ourselves. We will either resent the cross and walk away mad or accept the cross and go on freer to learn from God. Fundraising, with its victories and disappointments, can be a school of the Spirit.

SUCCESS FACTORS

Not that we should go looking for trouble. Focus on your mission. Holmes Bryan of Evangelical Development Ministries speaks of "Success Factors" by which you can evaluate yourself.[2] Seven factors go a long way to determining whether you succeed or fail to reach your goals. My list differs only a little from his.

1. Conviction about the call. The belief that what you are doing makes a critical difference for people, and the twin belief that Jesus has called you personally to undertake the job, is "the one thing most needed" (Lk 11:41). From sitting at Jesus' feet and hearing him speak flows everything else. Nourish that awareness of his call through all the means of grace available to you.

A major mission just surveyed fifty of its staff. Forty-nine did not have a prayer life consisting of anything more than preparing for lessons or Bible studies. Find the people in your mission who have warm hearts for the Lord beyond their "jobs." We can have intellectual conviction, willpower and cleverness without a real life of prayer, but we can't for long fake the presence of Jesus.

2. Asking. When you review your situation, ask yourself: In the last twelve months, how many people have I asked for gifts of $500 or more? If it's fewer than thirty, there's the problem.

3. Accountability. What will happen if we don't ask? No one raises support unless they have to. You and I are no exception. It's good when our organizations hold us to certain targets, but if they don't, we or our team should set them for ourselves.

4. Access to a network of people with ability and interest. We discussed access in chapters five and six. Again, it's nice if your agency helps to open doors. But if it can't or won't, and you really believe the work must get done, use the advice in those chapters and work your way there.

5. Support from your supervisor. Your supervisor needs to give you the time to build a support team and see that you get mentoring for the effort. Mentoring is not available in many lightly staffed ministries, so find someone—a fellow staff worker, a long-time donor, a person from another agency—who can go on calls with you at least once a year. Be prepared to make a case to your supervisor for taking the time you need.

6. A system to organize your information. See chapter eight.

7. Training. We don't know we need it until we get it, but then we say, "Wow, I wish I had known that a year ago." Everyone who raises money should get at least a day of classroom training once a year. If your agency doesn't offer training, find it from people you respect.

But success in building a support team does not come from a seven-part formula, even a religious formula. Fundraising is relational. Relational factors are set in a deeper context: the mystery of personality, which can't be controlled by a set of how-tos. Fundraising can be a school of the Holy Spirit only if we keep a perspective of love and mystery.

Love for our donors. If we pay attention, our donors will let us know their hopes for their relationship with us and our mission. Some will be our mentors. Some will be our friends. Some will pastor us, and some we will pastor. Some will see us just as a way to get good things done—which is honorable enough. All of them will be partners, but each in their own way. Take each into special consideration and treat them all according to their sacred uniqueness. We can't reduce trust, love or care to an equation. We can only say that over time they will sense if they are our partners or just our projects.

The presence of God. Deeper than the mystery of human personhood is the mystery of God himself. He is life's only absolute, and his authority extends to fundraising for ministry. Once in a while he lets us know that results are finally in his hands.

In the fall of 1977 we moved to the San Francisco Bay Area to supervise InterVarsity's work there. We had learned to trust the Lord for our own funds, but now we were responsible for fourteen other people. I was twenty-eight years old and had no training, no strategy and weak networks. We went into December needing double our normal month's funding. This was prior to the cyber age, and we would not get our reports until mid-January.

We held some ineffective meetings and prayed desperate prayers. After a Sunday service two weeks into the new year, I asked our pastor to pray for me because I could not cope with the pressure. He promised to pray and told me that God would meet the need. I can't explain what happened next: all anxiety left me; I was irrationally lighthearted. Something in me had been put to death by this word from God through my pastor. New life had taken its place. The following Tuesday the reports arrived. God had provided all we needed plus six dollars.

Every missionary we know has stories like this. Paying attention to Jesus is wiser than any principle, formula or method. He is in, with and under all our little attempts to follow him. This alone is firm: in acts of deliverance like the parting of the Red Sea, in times of instruction like the leveling of commandments at Sinai, in moments of disorientation like the wandering of the Israelites through the desert, he is with us. He loves ... he waits ... he knows ... he hears.

Are you willing to get sent? Make your motto Psalm 50:15: "Call upon me in the day of trouble; I will deliver you, and you will honor me." The road we are sent on is not smooth, but it goes Godward.

Appendix 1

Frequently
Asked Questions

I've asked everyone I know, and I'm stuck at fifty percent of my support level. How can I find more prospects?

It's normal to find yourself on a plateau from time to time. Here are some steps you can take when you're there.

Review this action list.

☐ Did I ask people personally, face to face, or only through a letter or group presentation? If we haven't met personally with our prospects, we're not done with the people we know. Take out your priority prospect list and go down the list.

☐ When I met with people, was I clear? What did I ask each person for? Did I make the need clear? How did I state the request? What next step did we agree on? Go over your list and check.

☐ If my cultural context means that someone else should ask, have I asked that person clearly to ask for me?

☐ Have I asked my current donors for introductions? Am I working with my core supporters to solve the problem or trying to do it all myself? Are we praying together, asking the Lord for solutions?

☐ Am I asking only those people within my comfort zone? Are there circles of people I could meet with if I was bolder? Ask everyone on your segmented prospect list, not just the priority list.

☐ Have I applied the church strategy of chapter six?

Weigh the alternatives. If you've done all these things faithfully, go to your organization and tell them the situation. If your agency cannot help you, try some intermediate steps. Continue to cultivate your passion and explore your alternatives creatively. Do you need to be on full-time support now, or could you work part time? Could you team with another person in ministry to share housing and other costs?

Could you find a church whose support would come in the form of a room in a member's home? That's a form of financial contribution.

Unless you're working in an isolated situation, the real question is one of time, not people. There are plenty of people to meet, just not people whom you are ready to ask today. That's why it's wise to use fifty percent of your first year's time to build your base. Just as in your ministry, to catch fish we have to go where the fish are.

Examine yourself. Comfort zone is often the real issue. We may feel like we have to be best buddies with people before we can ask, but that's not how donors see it. If your values are theirs, they'll give and *then* get to know you. When we get to the edge of our comfort zone, we find out what values we really hold. Are we just giving it a try, or are we committed no matter what? You can't fake that, and people will pick up what's in your heart. The real question could be, do you believe in what you're doing *strongly enough to take social risks?* When you have that conviction and are still stuck, wait on the Lord for his answer.

What about gifts from nonbelievers?

Few non-Christians will give to your work. Don't seek funds from them. The Christian character of many missions has been compromised through donor alliances with government, corporate or individual non-believers. One of our friends was recently offered a large grant if his inner-city agency would remove the name "Christian" because the foundation had a policy of not giving to religious causes. He refused, saying that "Christian" was the basis of all their work. The foundation actually gave the grant but wouldn't renew it in the future. "We're making an exception because you have the best tutoring program we've seen this year."

Third John 5-8 says,

> Dear friend, you are faithful in what you are doing for the brothers, even though they are strangers to you. They have told the church about your love. You will do well to send them on their way in a manner worthy of God. It was for the sake of the Name that they went out, receiving no help from the pagans. We ought therefore to show hospitality to such men so that we may work together for the truth.

"Receiving" could also be translated "accepting," which would imply the refusal of help offered from nonbelievers. But if we render the word as "receiving," then the text simply says that these Christians gave up normal sources of income (their jobs) for a cause no one but believers would appreciate.

Further, there are examples in Scripture of believers receiving material help from pagans. The Israelites asked Egyptians to give silver and gold to speed their exodus (Ex 12:35), Nehemiah asked King Artaxerxes to fund his mission of temple reconstruction (Neh 2:4-8), and Joanna, the wife of Herod's steward, passed along money likely acquired through his evil regime (Lk 8:3). When does money become clean enough for God to use? That's not always clear. Many missionaries tell of nonbelieving relatives and friends who offered help and, in some cases, became believers.

In any case, you'll find that it's basically the people of God who fund the work of God. Maybe the Lord is drawing your relatives to himself through your work. If they wish to help after you've presented what you do, accept their gift with thanks but don't count on it for the future. Don't say, "I could never take a check from you; you're not a Christian." But do turn down gifts that would link you to personalities or organizations that would influence you to compromise your distinctive as a

Christian. The father of one missionary owned a bar but the missionary thought it best not to list the Wild Nite Saloon as a ministry sponsor.

What about gifts from Roman Catholic and Orthodox churches?

"Make every effort to maintain the unity of the Spirit in the bond of peace" (Eph 4:3 NRSV). Emphasize our common ground but don't put money into the equation. It's more likely to be a source of friction than harmony.

Does the criteria of evangelical theology (see chapter six) mean that you should not seek financial support from these two historic churches? Unfortunately the answer at this time is yes. Justification by faith in the finished work of Jesus Christ is an evangelical distinctive, disputed by the Orthodox Church and understood differently in the Roman Catholic Church. Individual Catholics and Orthodox may support your work, but you'll discover that their churches give only to causes within their traditions. Show respect for those traditions by being honest about your own and not soliciting them.

You say support raising is relational. How can I find the time to have close relationships with donors, fellow staff and kids in my ministry?

A "close relationship" to a donor is not the same thing as a "close relationship" to a youngster, student or neighbor in your work. For a donor, close is four meetings a year to discuss your ministry. When you were in college, "close" meant hanging out three times a week.

Still, be sure you build that base in a church your first year before you become totally absorbed in direct ministry. If you're headed overseas, this won't be your problem, but if you're in campus or city work, it's a major issue. From your second year on, put in your thirty to forty days and save the rest for your work. Use your calendar and the contact plan system. Most of the trouble comes from not planning far enough ahead.

Finally, make sure your supervisor knows what kind of time and help you need to get the job done right. Some agencies schedule their interns too heavily to build a support base. If you can't seem to get the time you need, ask your pastor or lead donors to help your supervisor understand what's involved.

One of my donors offered me a matching gift. How should I respond?
Thank her and then get your donor in touch with your supervisor or agency headquarters to confirm her intent and set up the simplest procedure. Confirm the goals. For instance, is her gift to help you get to your full funding? Do a special project? Acquire something your ministry needs, such as a van or an office system? Draft a letter for the approval of both your donor and supervisor that you can send to your mailing list.

What qualifies as a matched gift? New contributors only, higher gifts from current donors or any gift during the current year? This can get technical real fast, which is another good reason to ask for help from your agency.

Enclose a reply envelope and mail it; then follow the standard procedure of following up with a phone call. If the gift affects other staff besides you, try to gather and phone as a group from a church or business. You'll be clearer and bolder as you ask.

A donor who runs a business offered to give me contacts in exchange for my prospect lists. How should I respond?
Turn him down. This "offer" not only violates your prospects' trust, it flunks the donor-motive test. It's not a partnership built on shared values. Don't be drawn into a discussion of why it's ethical and a great once-in-a-lifetime opportunity for you and your donors. This person is not out for your good. A polite "thank you" and "I'm not free to do that, and if you have any questions you can write to our headquarters" will do. Don't feel bad if he stops giving. In biblical terms, you're unequally yoked.

I'm about to phone the people on my lists, but a lot of them haven't heard from me in years. That feels so phony. What can I possibly say?
Say what's on your heart. Try, "I know we haven't talked in years. I'm now going out with a mission to Ulan Bator and need all the help I can get. Can I send you my request letter?" or "I know this is out of the blue,

but I'm going to work with at-risk teens in Philadelphia and need all the help I can get." If the Lord is calling you, he's calling people to help you. This is a great example that what we think as missionaries is so often not what our friends think as donors. Ironically, by *not* calling your old acquaintances, you are forfeiting the relationship. By calling them and risking, you'll gain relationships back. Check it out: most people will enjoy hearing from you.

What are stock gifts?

Stocks are no longer a way for just the upper class to build wealth or give. With the rise in stock market values of recent years, North America has developed a new "broad middle-income investor class." In 1997 more than forty percent of American adults owned $5000 or more of stocks. The percentage of stockowning families with incomes between $25,000 and $49,000 jumped almost 50 percent from 1989 to 1995— nearly one in two middle class families.[1] If these stocks are not held in a tax free or tax deferred account, they are subject to significant tax if sold. As a result, more donors want to use stocks instead of cash for their charitable giving.

Let's illustrate. Imagine Rita Donor bought one hundred shares of XYZ stock for $20 a share in 1995. Five years later it's worth $100 a share. Let's say also that Rita wishes to give to your ministry. If she sells her stock in the state of California, 80 percent—the "capital gain"—is taxable at 29 percent. Taxes eat up $2,480, and she can give the remaining $7,520 to your cause which she can deduct from her income tax. But if she gives the stock, she can avoid paying any tax at all, and deduct the entire value of the stock, $10,000. It's phenomenal.

In your case statement, list stock as a way to give. When a donor wishes to do so, put her in touch with your organization's finance office, and they will furnish instructions on how to transfer the stock from her account to your agency's and send her a receipt indicating the date of the gift and the number of shares given.

Ask your agency for its statement on how its friends can help with stock gifts.

Aren't the number of potential donors to my cause shrinking since the gap between rich and poor is widening? Aren't fewer families middle class?

Actually, while the gap is widening because of dramatic wealth creation at the top, more and more people are moving upward. The real question is income mobility over time. That is, do the poor tend to make it to the middle class? The University of Michigan's Panel Survey on Income Dynamics, regarded by some as the best documented study of the subject, tracked roughly 50,000 Americans over seventeen years. Of the people in the lowest fifth of income distribution in 1975, *only 5.1 percent were still there in 1991. Twenty-nine percent had made it into the highest fifth.*[2] As they say, past performance is no guarantee of future results, but the indications are that the number of potential donors is growing, not dwindling. After all, someone's been funding the explosion of non-profits.

And what about the poor? Are they not getting poorer? In 1994, households defined as poor by the government had more conveniences than the average household did in 1971.[3] If we consider hourly wages and benefits together, real compensation for jobs at the bottom of the ladder has increased 17 percent since the early 1970s.[4]

Consider this snapshot from "Reaching for the American Dream: A Multicultural Perspective" which was taken from a report to the White House on the Multicultural American Dream Index in 1998:

☐ African-American homes with annual incomes of over $100,000 tripled from 1994 to 259,000. African-Americans represent $400 billion in buying power.

☐ Latinos had 193,000 households with annual incomes over $100,000, and their purchasing power had tripled since 1973 to $270 billion.

☐ Women headed 220,000 households with income of $100,000 or more. Forty-two percent of Americans with gross assets of $600,000 or more were women, and 80 percent of the time women controlled household assets.[5]

These figures don't even account for assets such as homes. All this, even while North America draws many thousands of poor immigrants in each year and while divorce, a primary correlation to poverty, has become a national plague.

None of this, of course, denies the presence of racism, injustice, spiritual blindness or moral decline. It just says that if you want to do something about evil and need to raise funds to do it, the money is out there.

Appendix 2

Getting Sent on Short-Term Missions

GUIDANCE

Short-term missions lasting from two months to two years work best when the short-term missionary gets sent. When you start to feel the tug to get involved in a mission, float the idea with your friends, your Bible study group, your pastor and other mature Christians. Share what God is doing in your life. It might be a call from the Lord. It might just be a call to be open. Ask them to pray with and for you.

THE LOCAL CHURCH

You may have gathered that it's hard to do this without a local church. That's our intent. We don't believe in churchless, rootless short-termers. If you're not in a community of believers in your own culture, you are not ready to go to another culture. If you're desperate to build a building for someone, try a Habitat for Humanity project in your own city.

It's tempting to fund yourself if you have the means, but it is more biblical to stand before a missions committee or sit with a fellow

Christian and ask for their guidance and support. The same fund development principles apply to long-term and short-term ministry. Let's highlight the differences.

Guidelines
If you're sent out from a local church, they will likely have guidelines for you to follow for fundraising. If you are asking your church to fund your work with a certain mission agency, that agency will have materials for you to use. Normally that will include brochures, a budget sheet, perhaps a video and sample fundraising letters. Ask for a contact person in the agency to coach you periodically.

Timing
As the chapter on church explains, you'll need someone in the church structure, a missions committee person, elder or pastor, who can explain how to apply for support. Get in front of your church's budget deadlines. As soon as you are interested in short-term work, let the decision-makers know you are interested, and ask for input. "If I go with Mission XYZ for a year, do you think the church would fund my work? What would be the best way to approach the committee for financial help?" Don't wait to ask until you've put your plane ticket on your Visa card.

Plan B
If for some reason the church can't take you on, ask them to open an account or put a line item in their budget to which people can give. Make sure the accounting is handled by someone reliable. If it is, such an account is one way to involve your church and pick up support from people who want to help.

In any case, chapters six, twelve and thirteen are full of ideas for mobilizing your church's support.

AN EVENT, NOT A PROCESS

When your tour of duty is short, you are asking much less of donors.

People will more quickly commit to help with a one-time need than to begin an ongoing partnership. Because of this,

☐ Frame your case as a project. (What's the need? What will you do to help meet the need?)

☐ Your prospects, unlike the longer term worker, will not be the result of cultivation and development. You go on the contacts you have already. Put all the names, addresses, phone and e-mail numbers of your networks on a master list. See chapters two and five.

☐ Your budget will be smaller than a regular missionary's. It probably will not include insurance, health coverage or retirement plan. It will have some important one-time charges, however, such as travel to and from your field, costs of an orientation program, supplies and a budget to transport them to your field.

The meat of your budget is each project you will be doing, or each goal of your main project, with the dollar figure prorata's based on the percentage of time you think you'll need for it. This is preferable to the classic list of stipend, expenses and overhead. For example, let's say you are going to do a one year ministry in a Russian orphanage with children ages twelve to seventeen.

You are going because Russian orphans by law are released onto the street at age seventeen. They have no religious training, no way to make a living and no family to go to. Half of the boys are taken into organized crime, and at least half the girls into prostitution. Your case statement may be a simple brochure and some photos of these kids.

Your mission is to help give these kids a future by introducing them to Jesus Christ and educating them in a marketable skill. Your budget, then, could look like figure A.1.

On seeing your budget laid out as in figure A.1, a donor can be invited to fund or pray for a very specific part of your ministry. The dollar figure represents the true, full cost of delivering the program: your food, housing, insurance, materials—all of it.

Finally, *don't underbudget.* The biggest single mistake short-termers make is to minimize their expenses so they don't have to raise much money. Guess what: things go wrong overseas. Either you confront the fact that you have to ask for money and ask for enough of it, or you will come home in debt. Take your minimum budget and add 20 percent to each item.

Transportation		$ 2,500
Language Training		2,500
Orientation		900
Computer Training Program (Twenty-five Children)		12,000
Hardware ($3,000)		
Paper ($200)	subtotal:	3,200
Bible Classes (Thirty-five Children)		12,000
Materials ($200)		
Crafts ($300)	subtotal:	500
Evangelism Excursion to Oka River		3,000
Communications		600
Total for 2000-2001 Russia Orphans Ministry		**$37,200**

Figure A.1. Sample budget

COMMUNICATIONS

As a short-termer, you need to send at least three letters:
☐ the "first letter" described in chapter nine
☐ at least one letter from the field every six weeks you are there
☐ a report letter after you return

Every donor should receive a handwritten expression of thanks. This can be a sentence or two on your form letter or a separate postcard or thank-you stationery. The local postcard is a great device, even if some countries take a while to move them along the postal route.

Go easy on the e-mail. In developing countries access can be very limited and expensive. A short-termer in Guatemala stood in line two hours for the local phone. It was in a house. The homeowner had decided to go entreprenuerial, charging folks what the market would bear. The short-termer eventually got to pay his fee, plug his laptop modem into a port (lucky they had a modular port) and connect with home. Your host missionaries and other leaders are first in line in this kind of situation, so don't promise that you'll use e-mail to keep in touch. Ask your agency if it's available and if you should budget for it.

If you are gone more than a summer, you should have a volunteer stateside who manages your mailing list. The ideal is that you send your letter, and he or she formats, prints, stuffs the envelopes and sends. Ask your small group fellowship or Sunday-school class to help.

Most important, recruit a prayer leader who will gather a small group each month to pray for you. Short-term missions entail spiritual warfare.

Don't go there on your own—get sent.

Notes

Chapter 2: The Fear Factor
[1]Martin Seligman, *Learned Optimism* (New York: Simon & Schuster, 1991), pp. 43-50. In 1998 Seligman became president of the American Psychological Association.

Chapter 3: Why People Give
[1]Thom Grier, "The Philanthropist Next Door," *US News and World Report*, December 1997, p. 71.

[2]Gallup survey cited by Tim Stafford, "Anatomy of a Giver," *Christianity Today*, May 19, 1997, p. 22.

[3]Calvin O. Pressley is executive director of the Institute in Church Administration and Management of the Interdenominational Theological Center in Atlanta, Georgia.

[4]Calvin O. Pressley, "Financial Contributions for the Kingdom from the Elect: Giving Patterns in the Black Church," in *Cultures of Giving*, ed. Charles Hamilton and Warren Ilchman, New Directions for Philanthropic Fundraising (San Fransico: Jossey-Bass, 1995), pp. 96-99.

[5]Barry McLeish, *The Donor Bond* (Rockville, Md.: Fund Raising Institute, 1991), pp. 113-26.

[6]Stafford, "Anatomy of a Giver," p. 24.

[7]William D. Hautt, "Taking Donors Seriously," *Handbook for Young Life, Inc.* (Alemeda, Calif.: Focus Consultants, 1996), p. 6.

Chapter 7: Step Four: Prioritize
[1]*Wall Street Journal*, November 12, 1996, quoting Thomas Stanley and William Danko, *The Millionaire Next Door* (New York: Longstreet, 1996).

Chapter 9: Send Your First Letter
[1]Siegfried Vogele, cited in Dick Hodgson, "New Ideas and Techniques to Increase Response," *Potentials in Marketing* 26, no. 4 (1993): 67-69.

Chapter 10: Phone Your People
[1]Barry McLeish, "Resource Development in a Culture Shaping New Rules," presentation, June 1995.

Chapter 12: Ask for Church Support
[1]Rick Langeloh, "What the Church Expects of Missionaries," address to mission representatives, San Francisco, 1988.

[2]Tim Stafford, *The Friendship Gap* (Downers Grove, Ill.: InterVarsity Press), pp. 135-36.

[3]Langeloh, "What the Church Expects."

Chapter 16: Send Mail
[1]Ann Lamott, *Bird by Bird* (New York: Anchor, 1994), p. 19.

Chapter 17: Ask Again
[1]Kim Klein, *Fundraising for Social Change* (Berkeley, Calif: Chardon Press, 1996), p. 27.

Chapter 18: Get Sent for Good

[1]Martin Luther, *Lectures on Romans,* trans. Wilhelm Pauck, Library of Christian Classics (Philadelphia: Westminster Press, 1961), pp. 181-83; and *An Exposition of the Lord's Prayer,* trans. Martin Bertram, Luther's Works, vol. 42 (Philadelphia: Fortress, 1969), p. 44.

[2]Holmes Bryan, presentation to InterVarsity National Service Center, Madison, Wis., February 1991.

Appendix 1: Frequently Asked Questions

[1]Paul Gigot, "This Isn't What Marx Meant by Das Kapital," *Wall Street Journal,* March 20, 1999, p. A21.

[2]W. Michael Cox and Richard Aln, *Myths of the Rich and Poor* (New York: BasicBooks, 1999), pp. 72-77.

[3]Ibid, p. 15.

[4]Ibid, p. 19.

[5]Graham Gregory Bozell, Market Segment Research and DemoGraph Corp., cited in *American Demographics*, December 1998, p. 24. Bozell's figure for Asian Americans is almost certainly far too small. The now very dated 1990 census data set the number of Asian-American households with annual incomes of greater than $75,000 at forty-nine thousand—in the San Francisco Bay Area alone. Of these forty-nine thousand, 42.7 percent were ethnic Chinese and 24.4 percent were Filipino. These data are cited in Stella Shao, "Asian-American Giving," in *Cultures of Giving II,* ed. Charles Hamilton and Warren Ilchman, New Directions for Philanthropic Fundraising (San Francisco: Jossey-Bass, 1995), pp. 59-60.